Songs of Faith

Signs of Hope

Songs of Faith

Signs of Hope

David Poling

Word Books, Publisher
Waco, Texas

SONGS OF FAITH/SIGNS OF HOPE

Printed in the United States of America.

Library of Congress catalog card number: 75–36184

Table of Contents

Acknowledgments

Every book published has its unseen, and often, unheralded helpers. Therefore, my appreciation goes to those people in the warehouse, the packers, shippers, and other messengers that send it on its way. Also thanks to those who have set this type, read the proof-sheets, and designed the jacket. And forget not those who promote its very existence . . . helpers on whose skills we all depend.

Special thanks to personal friends at Word Books: Floyd Thatcher and Ron Patterson for their advice and encouragement along the way.

Also, to three individuals in Albuquerque, New Mexico, who gave enthusiastically of their time to the completion of this effort: Karen S. James, librarian, Menaul School Media Center, for thoughtful suggestions in bibliography; to Anna Mary Bogue, for her lifetime in music and her particular skills as a research specialist; to Lois H. Jackson, pastor's secretary of First United Presbyterian Church and music major who brought diligent and swift attention to a manuscript that became a book. To all, my deepest thanks.

David Poling

1975

Introduction

Music. What a large and significant part it plays in our lives—especially for those of us who are not gifted, who pick up our musical tastes and traditions in an almost casual, and, at times, careless manner. Yet we love music and we know what we like, no matter what the experts, professionals, and teachers tell us. Music has a message; it brings to us the sensations of romance, patriotism, melancholy, and inspiration. A song, a tune, reveals the moments of joy as well as the memories and flashbacks of other times and people. It is deeply personal and often social. For many, music marks the high points of human existence.

As I write this, a controversy is raging over country music, which jazz musician Stan Kenton has just labeled a "national disgrace." To a reporter from the *Nashville Banner,* Kenton remarked, "I hate country and western music. It is ignorant music and perverted music. I abhor it. . . . It is an absolute national disgrace and the lowest form of contemporary music." Earlier in the year jazz drummer Buddy Rich said that country music "appeals to intellectuals with the minds of four-year-olds."

Music has the power to divide as well as unite, to enrage as well as entertain. In the area of religious music and the songs covered in the first 200 years of American life, we have every taste and temperament represented. There will be some hymns here revered by all and a few despised by the "experts." Yet every one of them has meaning and a place in the lives of the people.

In preparing this book I discovered the sources of my own music history—mostly within the church. The major highlights of my childhood and youth were fashioned by the music of the Christian community. Who could forget the excitement of carols sung on a snowy Christmas morning in New Jersey—with the adult choir returning to the manse following their dawn caroling? Who could forget the carolers stomping into the house to see our tree, to down large cups of hot cocoa and devour plates of homemade doughnuts, and to sing more carols? What are the sounds of Christmas? The church and the music of children trying to get it together for the pageant and their parents; learning the first song, "Away in a Manger," giggling over the squeaky sounds of some—and marveling at the solo notes that came from your best friend who never told you he could sing like a woman; getting ready for the big evening, racing around empty classrooms with gowns flying, angels shouting, and directors groaning as the time of pageant neared.

The music of the church was expressed in all its tradition: liturgical and nonliturgical. It punctuated sermons and celebrations, combined childhood and youth, and gave us an entry into adulthood—because we soon learned *their* songs and shared their responses and sat all the way through the *Messiah,* experiencing firsthand the vibrating, chilling sensations that run up and down the backbone when a chorus launches into the "Hallelujah Chorus."

Gradually we learned different songs. Fellowship songs and gospel hymns meant Sunday evening and Wednesday night prayer meeting. Singing around the tables after family night suppers meant using the red hymnals (the green were used for Sunday morning).

And very early in our development we went to summer conferences and gulped the bright fresh air of the Rockies. We attended programs in New Mexico and Arizona and discovered that "conference songs" rated among the best. Can you imagine the excitement and grandeur of singing "Day Is Dying in the West" and actually being in the West?

Amid the awesome peaks, towering pines, and whoosh of evening vesper air, we concluded our day's program with worship. Music was live and life was music.

And in the Sandias, high above Albuquerque, we sat by a rushing stream and heard the first cowboy preachers speak to us of values beyond the clamor of youth. We stood together and thought we might be ascending when we sang "We Are Climbing Jacob's Ladder." And that vesper hillside in the West, East, South, or along the Columbia River in the North has a power and a memory—often because of the people we came to love and know. How thankful we are for the music that drifted so permanently into our lives and the lives of our friends. Those days have vanished. And many who laughed and played and prayed are gone. My own hair is now gray and the cowboy preachers have moved to a higher, eternal campground, not to be seen on this side of the spiritual divide. But the music remains and I believe. Faith continues and I love God for the music, for like his Son, it transcends time and eternity.

Music is a shared experience and that is, of course, what the Christian faith is all about. From the earliest accounts in the Old Testament we read that Moses and the people of Israel sang this song to the Lord saying:

> I will sing to the Lord, for he has triumphed
>   gloriously;
>   the horse and his rider he has thrown into
>   the sea.
> The Lord is my strength and my song,
>   and he has become my salvation
>   (Exod. 15:1–2).

In the biblical tradition there are songs of mourning, songs of lamentation, songs of celebration, and hymns of praise. There are songs for captivity, for as the psalmist records:

> By the waters of Babylon,
>   there we sat down and wept,
>   when we remembered Zion.

On the willows there
  we hung up our lyres.
For there our captors
  required of us songs,
and our tormentors, mirth, saying
  "Sing us one of the songs of Zion" (Ps. 137:1–3).

For believing people, songs were essential. A new song meant fresh information, reminders of past victories, moments to sing the Lord's praise.

The music in your life, if it is like mine, has been both planned and spontaneous, expected and unusual. One can still hear the music of the cowboy camp meetings, the great revivals, or the thunderous chorus of a chapel choir. It may be the lonely, loving ballad of a housewife on the prairie or the quartet of an evening service in Kentucky. Whether it be the hymns of a cathedral or the closing song at a summer campfire, music has power beyond measure, yet that is our task here: to measure, remember, and renew the religious tradition that stretches more than 200 years back into our national history.

1

Singing the Good News

Faithful people and devoted believers have always sung praises to God. This tradition flows from Jerusalem to Rome, from Geneva to Glasgow, from Holland to New Jersey. The perceptive historian of the fourth century, Eusebius, noted in his journal:

> The command to sing psalms in the name of the Lord was obeyed by everyone in every place. . . . In the whole church the people of Christ, who are gathered from all nations sing hymns with a loud voice.

And it was not just a regional experience or the special practice of those who resided in the Holy Land. Later, St. Ambrose would record:

> Each man does his utmost in singing what will be a blessing to all. Psalms are sung in the home and rehearsed on the streets. A psalm is learnt without labor and remembered with delight. Psalmody unites those who disagree, makes friends of those at odds, brings together those who are out of charity with one another.

The presence of the first hymns and religious songs in the

13

American settlement was the result of music sung in Europe. The ideas of religious liberty which bloomed in the American colonies had been planted earlier in the Puritan and pilgrim communities of Holland and England. The forms of worship and the sounds of praise had long been exercised on the other side of the Atlantic.

The first psalmbook cherished by the Puritans had been published by one of their own, Henry Ainsworth of Amsterdam. The Puritans had been using this book before, during, and after their arrival in the New World—as early as 1612. Dr. Ernest Ryden pictures the song fitting the sacrifice:

> Amid the storm they sang,
>   And the stars heard and the sea;
> And the sounding aisles of the dim woods rang
>   With the anthems of the free.

We should not be surprised that when John Alden sought the hand of Priscilla in marriage, that "open wide on her lap lay the well-worn psalmbook of Ainsworth."

But more than the covers were getting worn. Those persons shaping the American tradition in church music were apparently ready to create songs and hymns of their own. Two streams had flowed from Europe and England to fill the reservoir of American religious music: the "separatists" from Holland, and the orthodox singers from England who preferred the psalmbook of the established Church of England (as prepared by such leaders as Sternhold and Hopkins).

However, both of these traditions were ultimately to yield, like the Crown, to the inspiration of American psalmbooks which jumped back into history in order to be close to the original Hebrew of the Old Testament. The creation in 1640 of the *Bay Psalm Book* was a big event within the Christian community of the colonies. The editors must have sensed that their New World product would not receive thunderous applause for its style or literary grace, because in the preface they acknowledged:

If therefore the verses are not always so smooth
and elegant as some may desire or expect; let them
consider that God's altar needs not our polishings:
Exodus 20, for we have respected rather a plaine
translation, than to smooth our verses with the
sweetness of any paraphrase, and soe have attended
to conscience rather than elegance, fidelity rather
than poetry, in translating the Hebrew words into
English language, and David's poetry into English
meetre: that soe we may sing in Sion the Lords
songs of praise according to his own will; until hee
take us from hence, and wipe away our tears, and
bid us enter into our masters joye to sing eternal
Halleluiahs.

With that warning, those who published the *Bay Psalm
Book* pumped out nearly two dozen editions (and enjoyed extensive use back in the Old World as well). One example of
the metrical form and invisible poetry is found in Psalm 137:

> The rivers of the Babilon
>   there when wee did sit downe:
>   yea even then wee mourned, when
>   wee remembered Sion.
>
> Our harps wee did hang it amid,
>   upon the willow tree.
> Because there they that us away
>   led in captivitee,
> Required of us a song & thus
>   askt mirth: us waste who laid,
>   sing us among a Sions song,
>   unto us then they said.

This was psalm singing. It was heavy, unpolished, un-
poetical, yet prevailed in the early Christian community of
New England for nearly a century, or at least until Isaac
Watts in 1707 put together his volume, *Hymns and Spiritual
Songs.*

The excitement and vitality of the American pioneer experience was to break loose in the field of religious music as

much as in the yearning for political freedom or economic self-determination from England. The biggest boost for American hymn music came with the unfolding of the Great Awakening, the first major revival among the thirteen colonies.

At the center of this contagious spiritual awakening was the preaching of Jonathan Edwards, a New England Calvinistic clergyman who admitted that "it was really needful that we should have some other songs than the Psalms of David." Much of the fuel for the Great Awakening (which began in 1734) was the presence of George Whitefield from England and the general influence of John Wesley, who was Whitefield's mentor. Wesley had long since responded to the need and inspiration of congregational singing at his revivals, and this spilled over into the American experience.

The Revolutionary War and the preceding intensity of anti-British feeling brought a reaction against the old psalms and songs. The Reverend Joel Barlow, a chaplain in the Continental army, was asked to prepare a hymnal that would satisfy this nationalistic fervor. He gathered some seventy hymns and the collection was published during the war. However, this did not satisfy the whole religious community and it wasn't until Jonathan Edwards's grandson, Timothy Dwight, Yale president and Revolutionary chaplain, took up the assignment that things improved. Not only did Dwight inspire the troops with his own compositions but also edited a fresh version of Watts's *Hymns and Spiritual Songs* that was widely accepted.

Dwight was an extraordinary figure. As a preacher and educator he had a significant following in New England. As a hymn writer he reflected the new talent and freedom that flowed through the American system. In his editing of a hymnbook he gathered freely from many sources and was ecumenical in his selections: Cowper, Newton, Toplady, Charles Wesley and, of course, Watts. (Even with the recent anti-British sentiment, Dwight still incorporated 268 of Watts's hymns in his new edition!)

Dr. Ryden claims that Timothy Dwight, author of the famous hymn "I Love Thy Zion, Lord," was the "outstanding figure in the beginnings of American hymnody." Suffering from a severe visual disorder, the Yale president continued to give dynamic public leadership and untiring service to the church of Christ. His great hymn published in 1800 reflects his spirit and scope:

> I love Thy Zion, Lord,
> The house of Thine abode,
> The church our blest Redeemer saved
> With His own precious blood.
>
> I love Thy church, O God!
> Her walls before Thee stand,
> Dear as the apple of Thine eye,
> And graven on Thy hand.
>
> For her my tears shall fall;
> For her my prayers ascend;
> To her my cares and toil be given,
> Till toils and cares shall end.
>
> Beyond my highest joy
> I prize her heavenly ways,
> Her sweet communion, solemn vows,
> Her hymns of love and praise.
>
> Jesus, Thou Friend divine,
> Our Saviour and our King,
> Thy hand from every snare and foe
> Shall great deliverance bring.
>
> Sure as Thy truth shall last
> To Zion shall be given,
> The brightest glories earth can yield
> And brighter bliss of heaven.

Isaac Watts

The interplay of Isaac Watts and the building of an American tradition in religious music is one of the most profound events for the Christian church. Just as the hymnists in America were eventually to move away from the all-powerful Watts influence (just as they did from English government) so had Watts, in England, moved the singing of Christians away from the Calvinistic insistence that vocal music be entirely from the Psalms.

Watts gave the religious music world a foundation on which to build. The development in the United States away from the Watts domination did not mean that the church would ignore some of his finest hymns.

Watts was the breakthrough hymn writer who enabled the world Christian community to believe in its own talents and inspiration—especially the confines of biblical verse.

Watts (1674–1748) changed the shape of music in England and Europe. One of his most cherished hymns, "When I Survey the Wondrous Cross," can be traced to Paul's statement in Galatians 6:14. The argument here is that one does not have to be a Jew to become a Christian. So Paul states, "But far be it from me to glory except in the cross of our Lord Jesus Christ." As Albert Bailey comments in his *The Gospel in Hymns:*

> The cross is wondrous, because in this instance, a Roman instrument of torture and death, became God's instrument for saving mankind.

> When I survey the wondrous cross
>   On which the Prince of glory died,
> My richest gain I count but loss,
>   And pour contempt on all my pride.

> Forbid it, Lord, that I should boast,
>   Save in the death of Christ, my God;
> All the vain things that charm me most,
>   I sacrifice them to His blood.

> See, from His head, His hands, His feet,
>   Sorrow and love flow mingled down!
> Did e'er such love and sorrow meet,
>   Or thorns compose so rich a crown!

Were the whole realm of nature mine,
That were a tribute far too small;
Love so amazing, so divine,
Demands my soul, my life, my all.

ISAAC WATTS

Bailey traces at least a dozen Scripture references in this hymn which was written for use in communion services in 1707.

Watts was the source of thousands of hymns, all from the mind and frame of a most frail and sickly person. Brilliant in youth, he went on not only to churn out this vast hymn production, but to write dozens of books and treatises on grammar, theology, and psychology, as well as extensive collections of sermons.

Most famous of his hymns in America and common to almost all denominational hymnals are, "There Is a Land of Pure Delight," "Jesus Shall Reign Where'er tne Sun," "Joy to the World, The Lord Is Come," "Our God, Our Help in Ages Past."

Our God, Our Help in Ages Past

Our God, our Help in ages past,
Our Hope for years to come,
Our Shelter from the stormy blast,
And our eternal Home:

Before the hills in order stood,
Or earth received her frame,
From everlasting Thou art God,
To endless years the same.

A thousand ages in Thy sight
Are like an evening gone;
Short as the watch that ends the night
Before the rising sun.

Time, like an ever-rolling stream,
Bears all its sons away;

They fly forgotten, as a dream
Dies at the opening day.

Our God, our Help in ages past,
Our Hope for years to come,
Be Thou our Guard while life shall last,
And our eternal Home.

ISAAC WATTS

Watts was sensitive to the tensions and hopes of his time. "Our God, Our Help in Ages Past" was written in 1714, a most crucial period for British history. Protestant Queen Anne seemed disposed to permit extensive Roman Catholic influence in England—herself the daughter of James II, a Catholic. Many feared that the gains enjoyed by Dissenters and Reformers under the Act of Toleration would be swept aside by the advisers who surrounded the throne and were Roman in persuasion. On Sunday, August 1, 1714, Queen Anne died suddenly and was succeeded by Protestant George I. The alarms and anxieties of the people (at least Protestant) were not fulfilled and their sense of joy and celebration can be seen in "Our God, Our Help in Ages Past." This moving hymn of rejoicing and assurance spread widely throughout the Christian world. It is considered by many in Great Britain to be almost a second national anthem.

Newton and Cowper, from England to America, with Love

No two British hymnists are more closely related than John Newton and William Cowper. Their musical influence would extend far from England into the American frontier faith, carried on the wave of evangelistic crusades and camp meetings. John Newton was born in 1725, six years before Cowper. His life and pursuit of non-Christian interests and habits are rather well told by the epitaph resting today on his grave marker:

JOHN NEWTON, clerk, once an Infidel and Libertine, a servant of slavers in Africa, was, by the rich Mercy of our Lord and Savior Jesus Christ,

> preserved, restored, pardoned, and appointed to
> preach the Faith he had long labored to destroy.

Newton's life had been the sea, as was his father's. He detested this life, especially after being impressed into the British navy which he deserted only to suffer recapture and flogging at the mast.

For a time he served with a slaver, later becoming a captain and dealer in the miserable business of buying and selling humans. After six years of struggling with this degrading life, and reading the Christian classic, *The Imitation of Christ,* Newton fell in with a devout sea captain who helped him to conform his deep intentions of finding a better life and even pursuing his mother's wish of the ministry.

Through association with Wesley and Whitefield in Liverpool, he went on to study Hebrew and Greek, becoming a great student of the Bible. Finally, in 1764 he was ordained curate at Olney.

Newton's hymns are well known and are still among the most popular in the Christian world. "Amazing Grace, How Sweet the Sound" has come to be one of the most widely sung hymns of the twentieth century, reappearing in mainline denominational hymnals as well as identifying with the Billy Graham Crusades.

The words of this hymn, written by one who struggled through all the bonds of depravity to find Christian pardon and deliverance, are vivid indeed.

> Amazing Grace how sweet the sound
> That saved a wretch like me,
> I once was lost, but now am found
> Was blind, but now I see.

Newton was noted for some famous conversions (he preached beyond his eightieth year) but is perhaps best remembered for his supportive friendship and sheltering care of another hymn writer, William Cowper. For an almost intolerable existence, Cowper endured deep inclinations to commit suicide and was institutionalized at least four times with mental breakdowns. He dreaded insane asylums, feared life, and struggled for sixty-nine years with a desire to kill himself. Yet he had times of brilliant spiritual insight, was stabilized through his friendship with Newton, and produced with him the volume of Olney hymns.

Cowper wrote some of the most beloved hymns of the Christian library. He broke through his compulsions (he stammered and lisped) when addressing religious themes and gave to the millions that followed some of the most uplifting and inspiring songs of the faith. Sometimes Cowper would write a hymn after a suicide attempt had failed. He determined to throw himself into a river one night but the cab in which he was riding could not find the river because of dense fog. Disgusted, Cowper ended up at home. It was quite an evening because Cowper had first tried to drown himself, then he returned home to use a rope—which parted; and in final anguish, he fell upon a knife blade—which broke! Then came the lovely hymn, "God Moves in a Mysterious Way His Wonders to Perform."

"There Is a Fountain Filled with Blood" is in many of our hymnals today. Cowper wrote, "O for a Closer Walk with God," "Jesus, Where'er Thy People Meet," and "Sometimes a Light Surprises."

The tune we use most often to, "There Is a Fountain Filled with Blood," was written by Lowell Mason. Over the years some people have been put off by the first line but it does impart a strong message reflecting the struggle of the author.

> There is a fountain filled with blood
> Drawn from Emmanuel's veins;
> And sinners, plunged beneath that flood,
> Lose all their guilty stains.

The fifth stanza has the powerful reference to Cowper's personal experience with the redemptive power of God.

> When this poor lisping, stammering tongue
> Lies silent in the grave,

> Then in a nobler, sweeter song
> I'll sing Thy power to save . . .

It has been said that the soldiers of the Civil War were the "singing-est" soldiers in American history. More songs from that conflict between the states have endured than from any other war in American history. Some of the popular songs include, "Home, Sweet Home," "Pop Goes the Weasel," "Annie Laurie," and "Auld Lang Syne." The religious favorites abound: "Old Hundred," "All Hail the Power of Jesus' Name," "Amazing Grace," "I'm a Pilgrim," "Rock of Ages," "How Firm a Foundation" and "Nearer My God to Thee." In one review we have this account:

> On a few occasions soldiers sang together. When Confederate Private Goodwin got religion at one of the war time revivals, about fifty of his comrades accompanied him to the Rapidan River for baptism. The assembly aroused the curiosity of the Federals across the river and a number of them came to the bank to view the ceremony. When the Confederates began singing, "There is a Fountain Filled with Blood," the Federals chimed in, after which the convert was immersed to the satisfaction of all.
>
> from *They Who Fought There*

Ernest Ryden quotes Bishop Moule with this account of the death of William Cowper:

> About half an hour before his death, his face, which had been wearing a sad and hopeless expression, suddenly lighted up with a look of wonder and inexpressible delight. It was as if he saw his Savior, and as if he realized the blessed fact, "I am not shut out of Heaven after all!" This look of holy surprise and of joyful adoration remained until he had passed away. . . .

Newton and Cowper were almost inseparable in their later years. Newton, the old sea captain, would write in

1779, "Glorious Things of Thee Are Spoken," and "Zion City of Our God" with the music composed in 1797. These two men were united in life by their affection for Christ and their commitment to the church. In time they are linked to all those who have endured unimaginable distress, shame, and difficulty and have been, by the grace of God, victorious. Their hymns speak of such a triumph.

In her poem, "Cowper's Grave," Elizabeth Barrett Browning wrote:

> O poets, from a maniac's tongue was poured the
> deathless singing;
> O Christians, at your cross of hope a hopeless hand
> was clinging!
> O men, this man in brotherhood your weary paths
> beguiling,
> Groaned only while he taught you peace, and died
> while you were smiling.

The anti-British feeling among American colonists may have spilled and caused their rejection of English hymn writers—yet the tradition and power of Christian music were stronger than either nationalism. One important combination of lyricist/composer was that of Reginald Heber and Lowell Mason.

Heber was internationally famous as the missionary bishop to India (which may have heightened his acceptance in America) and was universally acclaimed for his outstanding hymns. "Holy, Holy, Holy" has been sung since 1826. "From Greenland's Icy Mountains" is regarded by many as the most enduring song for missions. Heber reflects here his poetic skills—which were recognized at an early period by such greats as Tennyson and Sir Walter Scott. The impact of his sixteen years in parish life in England was widely and enthusiastically received. Thackeray was known to have said that Heber was "one of the best of English gentlemen."

Yet, this best of the English church elite required the composition of a young bank clerk in America to put his hymn

into the hearts of Christian people everywhere. A woman
in Georgia sent some of Heber's material to Lowell Mason,
noted for his composing skills. Tradition has it that Mason
hammered out the tune of this missionary hymn "Greenland's Icy Mountains" in less than an hour! Apparently
Mason had this extraordinary knack of teaming up with able
lyricists and bringing forth stunning combinations. Mason
was to have a powerful and far-reaching career in post-
colonial America. Historians recall that Mason was walking
in downtown Boston when he bumped into Ray Palmer,
another church musician. Palmer was an established poet as
well as a Congregational preacher. Mason asked him if he
had any material for him to write some music. The Bostonian responded on the spot by producing a poem which
he was carrying around in a notebook.

Mason was fast—but not fast enough to produce the music
on the spot; yet, he returned several days later with the famous tune that is called "Olivet" and sung to "My Faith
Looks Up to Thee."

> My faith looks up to Thee,
> Thou Lamb of Calvary,
>   Saviour divine!
> Now hear me while I pray,
> Take all my guilt away,
> O let me from this day
>   Be wholly Thine.
>
> May Thy rich grace impart
> Strength to my fainting heart,
>   My zeal inspire;
> As Thou hast died for me,
> O may my love for Thee
> Pure, warm, and changeless be,
>   A living fire!
>
> When life's dark maze I tread,
> And griefs around me spread,
>   Be Thou my Guide;
> Bid darkness turn to day,

Wipe sorrow's tears away,
Nor let me ever stray
    From Thee aside.

When ends life's transient dream,
When death's cold, sullen stream
    Shall o'er me roll,
Blest Saviour, then, in love,
Fear and distrust remove;
O bear me safe above,
    A ransomed soul.

RAY PALMER

We may be giving the impression that Mason in his composition, and Palmer in his poetry were clicking off this creative work with casual spontaneity. That may be true but what must be remembered is that these were devout, intense artists who had steeped their lives in the faith and had immense affection for what they wrote and composed. To them, the creative surge was a gift of God and the expression, while swift, was the result of years of prayer and praise, alone and with others.

Palmer was a descendant of that pious New England pair, John Alden and Priscilla. His own days had been wracked with poverty and stress. At thirteen he had to seek employment to make ends meet, and only by the support and intervention of friends was he able to attend Phillips Andover Academy and later Yale. The phrase, "When life's dark maze I tread and griefs around me spread," arose from some very difficult times. In a later journal he confided about this hymn:

> I gave form to what I felt, by writing [he was teaching in Manhattan at the time] with little effort, the stanzas. I recollect I wrote them with very tender emotion and ended the last lines with tears.

Apparently, "My Faith Looks Up to Thee" had been part

of a devotional notebook that Palmer used regularly for private prayers. Only when approached by Mason in Boston several years later did this persuasive hymn come into being.

Palmer was really a man of great depth. He believed that his hymns were inspired and was known to have consistently refused payment for their use. He did, however, become greatly irritated when people attempted subtle changes in phrases or alteration of sentence structure.

Much of Palmer's works centered on the Lord's Supper. "Jesus, Thou Joy of Loving Hearts" is an immediate example of this New England piety—and good piety it was. He once wrote regarding his fondness of this theme:

> When the cares and business of life have hurried me hither and thither with no little distraction of mind, I love to come back again, and sit down before the cross, and gaze on the blessed Sufferer with silent, tender memories. It is like coming once more into the sunshine after long walking through gloom and mist.

Like other writers, Palmer had reached back into the twelfth century and made good use of the expression from the hand and heart of Bernard of Clairvaux. This may be the most representative refrain of the Middle Ages, powerfully regarded by David Livingston in his missionary trials, and made American through the gentle spirit of Ray Palmer.

People like Palmer, Mason, and Thomas Hastings did much to consolidate the hymnal gains of the churches within America as music moved into the advance of the nineteenth century. It is surprising to recall that psalms and hymns widely accepted in one period should be swept away so thoroughly in the next. But such was the ferment, excitement, and artistic yearning of the religious community in America. (For instance, Ainsworth's *Psalter,* once the absolute standard and then superseded by the *Bay Psalm Book* of 1640, had only one hymn to survive in later editions!)

The place and power of music within the church have been recognized in almost every century of its existence. It was Henry Ward Beecher who exclaimed:

> Hymns are the jewels which the Church has worn, the pearls, the diamonds, the precious stones formed into amulets more potent against sorrow and sadness than the most famous charm of the wizard or the magician. . . .
> And he who knows the way that hymns flowed, knows where the blood of true piety ran . . . and can trace its veins and arteries to the very heart.

William Billings (1746–1800), the composer who attracted the most attention during the latter part of the eighteenth century in the field of church music, was born in Boston and was by trade a tanner. Although he had little formal education, he was fired with an irrepressible zeal for developing popular singing. He was blind in one eye, had a withered arm, and one leg was shorter than the other, but he possessed a starling stentorian voice that drowned out all those near him.

Billings's first tune-book, *The New-England Psalm-Singer,* was published in 1770. His defiance of the rules of composition (which he had never bothered to learn) was expressed in the preface:

> Perhaps it may be expected by some, that I should say something concerning Rules of Composition; to these I answer that *Nature is the best Dictator,* for all the hard dry studied rules that ever were prescribed will not enable any person to form an air, any more than the bare knowledge of the four and twenty letters and strict grammatical Rules will qualify a Scholar for composing a piece of Poetry. . . . For my part, as I don't think myself confined to any Rules for Composition laid down by any that went before me, neither should I think (were I to pretend to lay down rules) that any who come after me were in any ways obliged to adhere

to them, any further than they should think proper; so in fact I think it best that Every Composer should be his own Carver.

This collection, and the five which followed it, contained his own compositions. They furnished, under his leadership, a colonial counterpart to the rise of Methodist singing in England. His tune, "Chester," with its defiant text became a veritable national anthem during the Revolutionary War.

The enthusiasm for the revolutionary cause pumped incessantly through the words and music of Billings. This rugged and aggressive New Englander was as eager to promote his material as he was to write and compose it. Early publications included *The Singing Master's Assistant* which appeared in 1778. The composition, "Chester," emerged as one of the most popular in the colonies, being sung in schools, churches, and wherever marching bands could gather. Billings intended his work to be used in the new "singing schools" and "Chester" was considered a favorite:

> Let tyrants shake their iron rods
> And slavery clank her galling chains.
> We fear them not, we trust in God,
> New England's God forever reigns.
>
> Howe and Burgoyne and Clinton, too
> With Prescott and Cornwallis joined,
> Together plot our overthrow,
> In one infernal league combined.
>
> When God inspired us for the fight,
> Their ranks broke, their lives were forced,
> Their ships were shattered in our sight,
> Or swiftly driven from our coast.
>
> The foe comes on with haughty stride,
> Our troops advance with martial noise;
> Their veterans flee before our youth,
> And generals yield to beardless boys.
>
> What grateful offering shall we bring

> What shall we render to the Lord?
> Loud hallelujahs let us sing,
> And praise his name on every chord!

Billings was skillful and fresh in his compositions for con-gregations. He relied on a text from Isaac Watts when he de-veloped these rounds which appeared in *The New-England Psalm-Singer.* Explained Billings in that publication:

> It is well known that there is more variety in one piece of fuguing music than in twenty pieces of plain song, for while the tones do most sweetly coincide and agree the words are seemingly en-gaged in a musical warfare. . . . Each part seems determined by dint of harmony and strength of accent, to drown his competitor in an ocean of harmony, and while each part is thus mutually striving for mastery, and sweetly contending for victory, the audience are most luxuriously enter-tained, and exceedingly delighted. . . . O enchant-ing! O ecstatic! Push on, push on ye sons of harmony!

He wrote:

> Thus saith the high the Lofty One
> I sit upon my holy throne,
> My name is God, I dwell on high
> Dwell in my own eternity.

A better-known round written by Billings is, "When Jesus Wept." It was designed for four voices, but could be sung by as few as two.

> When Jesus wept the falling tear
> In mercy flowed beyond all bound,
> When Jesus groaned a trembling fear
> Seized all the guilty world around.

A hymn of celebration, for victory in the Revolutionary War, and designed for civilians and soldiers alike, was

William Billings's, "Victory." It was a blend of his style and the words of Isaac Watts (who must have been amazed to ever know that his material would be applied to a war against Great Britain!).

> To thine almighty arm we owe the triumphs of the
> day
> Thy terrors, Lord, confound the foe, and melt their
> strength away.
> Tis by thine aid our troops prevail, and break
> united powers
> Or burn their boasted fleets! Or scale the proudest
> of their towers!

Denominational Sources for American Religious Music

We are all aware that every denomination and sect have their own style of hymns and music. What is not clear is the impact and effect that such music has had on other groups, especially those within the wider Christian fellowship. The New England influence, so heavily Calvinistic, was the initial leader in the musical development of America. Yet we have seen that it, too, went through substantial changes and alterations.

In his superior lecture series at Southwestern University some thirty years ago, Dr. Robert Guy McCutchan listed three key words which describe the stages through which American hymnody has passed:

Authority: that power derived from opinion, respect esteem, or long established reputation, such as the authority of primacy, example, or prestige. (Here the setting was complete in the first years of the American colonies as they imported ideas and methods from the countries of Europe and Great Britain.)

Anarchy: confusion or disorder in general; the assertion of individual liberty; license or the absence of regulatory powers. (This was the long period of ferment and transition as the religious groups in the colonies began to work out of old-world forms and began experimenting with large ideas such as freedom and self-determination.)

Insight: intellectual discernment; understanding; penetration; the power of seeing into a situation; a reflective knowing. (As time and events passed and the civilization of the United States took form, the many branches of the religious community gained a perspective on worship and a feel for new vitality in musical expression that was distinctly American.)

A most handy illustration of the first stage is seen in the writings of Longfellow in his *Courtship of Miles Standish* where Priscilla, awaiting the fabled visit of John Alden, gives us this scene:

> Open wide on her lap lay the well-worn psalm-
> book of Ainsworth,
> Printed in Amsterdam, the words and music to-
> gether,
> Rough hewn, angular notes, like the stones in the
> wall of a church yard,
> Darkened and overhung by the running vine of the
> verses.

Those Amsterdam printers would have to yield to the Boston publishers and the "stones in the wall of a church yard" would not go up as fast or far as the tents which sheltered the camp meetings along the frontier. As American frontier tastes emerged and the religious adventurers hit the road, hymns and gospel songs developed to mark both the pace and the theology of the people. It was a long way from the old established forms of London or the psalm-sounds of Amsterdam. But it was American, it was religious, and most frequently Christian.

The Unitarians were among the first to tinker with the hymnbooks of traditionalists, according to McCutchan. They were all over the Boston area, many in Congregational churches, and willing to add the work of Tate and Brady

who had created a hymnal known simply as "New Version."
This was around 1753.

Presbyterians—established, conventional, and comfortably
close to Calvin—had many difficulties when it came to the
development of music. Psalms were like gravity—powerful
and taken for granted; not to be doubted or manipulated.
Yet the booming force of the Great Awakening brought a
host of new musical happenings, especially with the preaching of Jonathan Edwards and George Whitefield. While
trained and associated with Wesley, Whitefield did not share
the taste for the development of hymns in place of psalms.
Yet the Great Awakening vaulted over their differences and
created a whole new arena for music and religious expression. The Presbyterians were plunged into a doctrinal hassle
over this psalm-hymn disagreement, ending with a split in
1741 over the "right" use. The result was the Old Side and
the New Side, a gathering into new synods. They did re-
unite eventually, but music showed its muscle more than
once.

It appears that Samuel Davies, president of what was to
become Princeton University, hacked away at the psalm-
singing stronghold of his own denomination—Presbyterian—
by writing some evangelistic hymns, "Lord, I am Thine,
Entirely Thine." Earlier, Davies had been a frontier missionary in Virginia—again the effect of the expanding wilder-
ness on the established patterns of the church and their
worship.

The Baptists (who shared a New England start with the
other Christian bodies) issued their own *Hymns and Spiritual
Songs* at Newport in 1766. Dr. McCutchan in his *Hymns in
the Lives of Men* has this reflection concerning the influence
of this denomination on America:

> Opening with sixteen hymns on baptism, this
> book became the first truly denominational hymnal
> in America. Yet there was a decided preference
> among Baptists for a more popular type of church
> song. Their recruits came from uncultured groups

gained through evangelistic methods; literary standards were not taken into account. Their preaching was highly emotional; and they wanted and developed a type of hymn in keeping with the character of the preaching—a fervid hymn which might be sung to a popular melody, preferably one with a refrain or chorus.

While the Baptists used Watts in New England, the southern and westward expansion brought in a new, dynamic style of singing.

2

Singing in the Spirit

"One of the striking features of the Reformation, both Protestant and Catholic, was the fashion in which it found expression through hymns. Indeed, it seems to have been true of most and perhaps all of the great forward surges of the Christian tide."

Kenneth Scott Latourette
History of Christianity

"I wept at the beauty of your hymns and canticles, and was so powerfully moved at the sweet sound of your Church singing. These sounds flowed into my ears, and the truth streamed into my heart."

St. Augustine
Confessions

"At the stroke of seven, several pleasant-looking men mounted the platform at the south end of Times Square. One of the men took his place at an organ, another at the piano on the platform. A wavy-haired man with an athletic build stood, raised his arms, and on the down-beat, 2000 people burst forth in song:

This is my story, this is my song;
Singing His praises all the day long."

from Billy Graham and the New York Crusade

Sankey and Moody

We have already commented on the increasing influence of the revivals and crusades in shaping the direction of American religious music. Personalities around these events came to have massive influence on the Christian church in Great Britain as well as America. Any consideration of the impact of the Dwight L. Moody and Ira Sankey revivals is to note that these American-born evangelists were as successful in England, Scotland, and Ireland as they were in the United States. Throughout the English-speaking world their gospel preaching and their enthusiasm for fresh, soul-stirring hymns became a trademark of their public image.

Before considering some of the hymns that gained extraordinary popularity in conjunction with their mass meetings, we ought to reflect on the reason for the surging power of the gospel songs in the United States.

1. In the early and middle decades of the nineteenth century (Moody, 1837–1899, and Sankey, 1840–1908) folk songs, ballads, spirituals, and hymns were a primary medium of communication for millions of people. On the growing, sprawling frontier, radio was a century away; books terribly expensive; newspapers were a once-in-awhile experience. It sometimes took weeks, even months, for people to learn of a war ended; a peace signed; a treaty ratified.

Therefore, songs were written to celebrate victories, to commemorate thrilling events, to proclaim and sustain the Christian faith—and a veritable river of words and music churned across the landscape. Christian believers in small towns and villages, folk making their way across bayous and plains, sang their faith as often as they voiced their prayers.

2. Hymns and gospel songs became the companions of peo-

ple who were sick or in trouble, in loneliness or sorrow. Church leaders employed music as a source of teaching and as an instrument of moral advocacy for a generation struggling with the wildness that accompanies a new nation with a provisional culture and a fledgling civilization.

The new excitement of booming cities and advancing frontiers also devoured men and women unaccustomed to the perils of gambling, the accessibility of abundant liquor, and the charms of every known vice. A rootless, often footloose, family-separated society had to be anchored down to something that had persuasive and convincing personal ethics.

So churchmen, lay and ordained, stabilized and supported vast millions of mobile believers through the ministry of the circuit rider, the appearance of the tent meetings, the impact and excitement of the itinerant evangelist. And there were lots of every kind. By the end of the nineteenth century, and riding on the wave crest of the Sankey–Moody revivals, there were at least 650 "minor league" evangelists in the United States alone.

3. The favored music of the camp meetings and the cherished songs of the revivals worked as well in urban areas as prairie ball parks. The response to the preaching of Dwight L. Moody in London and the songs of Sankey in Edinburgh, Scotland, was as great as their downtown meetings in Chicago and in the reworked warehouse in Philadelphia. Preaching and hymns, invitation and song simply did not wear out as long as people hurt, mothers feared, and men were lonely. The remembered music underscored the forgotten text or the preacher's tone. When the meetings were over and the tents folded, the Moody influence at last institutionalized in the Northfield schools of Massachusetts and Chicago, the songs were still sung and the mood relived with fresh force.

When publishers announced that the Moody–Sankey hymnbooks may have totaled more than fifty million, we sense the far-reaching extent and enduring quality of their ministry. The point is not that this form may not be our style and choice. The point is that it represented the longings and commitment of countless people, and became the central expression of the church in North America—and in many places of the English-speaking world. A visit to Australia and New Zealand today and many parts of Asia, Africa, Japan, and the Middle East prove the staying power of this religious musical expression.

One of the favorite hymns of Ira Sankey—and one of the favorite stories that he enjoyed telling—was the source for the hymn, "The Ninety and Nine" with words written by Elizabeth Clephane. Sankey had been on one of his extensive travels with Moody, riding on an all-night train from Glasgow to Edinburgh. Their evening was filled with the need to open mail, deal with correspondence, and plan for the next series of meetings.

Moody turned to the mail. Sankey opened a newspaper and read most of the evening. Several times he came back to the page which had a poem by a Scottish writer, Elizabeth Clephane, entitled, "The Ninety and Nine." Sankey tore it out and stuck it in his pocket.

Several years earlier, in 1865, this thirty-five-year-old Christian writer had composed, "Beneath the Cross of Jesus." Sankey probably knew this hymn, and may have been struck by the poignancy of the material that he found in the evening paper. The next revival was held with Moody preaching on a new text and theme, and Sankey unprepared with any special music to fit the event.

On the spur of the moment and the inspiration of the hour, he whipped out the newspaper clipping and produced a tune on the spot. Moody and others of the gospel team were amazed at this new song, and afterwards asked Sankey where he got it. He simply pointed to yesterday's paper and the persuasive poem of one Elizabeth Clephane. Miss Clephane wrote:

There were ninety and nine that safely lay

In the shelter of the fold.
But one was out on the hills away
Far from the gates of gold.
Away on the mountain wild and bare,
Away from the tender Shepherd's care.

Elizabeth and her sister served tirelessly the poor and destitute of Melrose. The words and emotion of her hymns reflected the inner love and compassion that she felt for the lost. Miss Clephane died at thirty nine. Her hymns remain as two of the most popular of the Christian community around the world.

Music Related to the Revival/Frontier Period of American Life

Songs were not only religious and devotional, but also served to implant morals in the lives of wayward youth. As a teaching vehicle, they were part of the remembered doctrines of the frontier church and reinforced the pious commitment of those who wrote and taught them. One example, published in a Boston collection, went straight to the point, "Miss Hathaway's Experience."

That dareing sin I did commit,
Was that, which some delight in yet,
That heinous sin called civil mirth,
God threatens with his dreadful curse.
I often-times to church did go,
My beauty and fine clothes to show.

The theme moves along with the change of heart and repentance of the young sinner, so at last she sings:

My uncle said, don't be so dull,
Come, go with me to yonder ball;
I'll dress you up in silks so fine,
I'll make you heir to all that's mine.

The Sunday school material of their nineteenth-century period in the United States comprised a heavy investment

in songs for children and youth to memorize. Religious publishing houses put out a powerful torrent of printed sheets
and booklets, incorporating new hymns written by composers
such as Stephen Foster. He wrote hymns for the funeral
services of children and youth, reflecting not only on the
theology of the time but also the perils of accidents and the
frequency of illness for the families of the new nation.

One of Foster's tunes said:

> Little Willie's gone to heaven,
> Praise the Lord!
> All his sins have been forgiven,
> Praise the Lord!
>
> Joyful let your voices rise,
> Do not come with tearful eyes,
> Willies dwelling in the skies,
> Willie's gone to heaven.

For little girls, Stephen Foster wrote this sentiment:

> Little Ella's an angel in the skies,
> Sing, merrily sing.
> Come brother and sister, cease your sighs,
> Sing, merrily sing.
>
> Sing, merrily sing,
> Let the chorus joyfully ring!
> Ella's an angel in the skies,
> Sing, merrily sing.

The dimensions of Christian theology and the mood of the
pioneer church are clearly implanted in the gospel music of
the 1800s. While it may not be our style or point of reference
as far as twentieth-century Christian doctrine is taught today, it is honest to that era. As Waldo Seldom Pratt concluded, "It constituted a historic phenomenon."

Charles Wesley produced a whole book, *Hymns for Children*. His theology was good for children as well as for adults:

> And am I only born to die?

And must I suddenly comply
With nature's stern decree?
What after death for me remains?
Celestial joys, or hellish pains,
To all eternity!

Great Revival Hymns

"Just As I Am" ranks with "How Great Thou Art" in the services conducted by evangelists today. Yet it was Dwight L. Moody who stated that "Just As I Am" probably touched more listeners and brought more people to Christ than any other song in the Christian library of gospel music.

Out of suffering—both physical and spiritual—this song was born. Charlotte Elliott was an invalid all of her eighty-two years. Born in 1789, she lived all of her life in England and wrote this piece in 1836—it first appeared in the *Christian Remembrancer* of which Miss Elliott was to later serve as an editor. Regarding her physical torments, she once wrote:

> He knows and He alone, what it is, day after day, hour after hour, to fight against bodily feelings of almost overpowering weakness, languor and exhaustion, to resolve not to yield to slothfulness, depression, and stability, such as the body causes me to long to indulge, but to rise every morning determined to take for my motto: If a man will come after Me, let him deny himself, take up his cross daily, and follow Me.

Miss Elliott chose to challenge the crunch and travail of her physical shortcomings and resolved to live with these words:

> God sees, God guards, God guides me. His grace surrounds me, and His voice continually bids me to be happy and holy in His service, just where I am.

It was the haunting theological struggle for a sense of per-

sonal salvation which gave Charlotte Elliott her greatest
torment—and which finally yielded to the persuasive teaching and conversation of the famous Swiss preacher, Dr.
Caesar Malan. Her brother, a minister in the Church of
England, entertained the noted cleric in their home in
Brighton, England. Here in 1822, Malan arrived from Geneva
and before he left convinced Miss Elliott that she was on
the wrong theological journey: she could do nothing on her
own merit to gain the grace of God. It was a gift. Up to now,
she believed that she must earn her redemption, merit salvation in order to become acceptable to God. "You have nothing
of merit to bring to God," he argued. "You must come just as
you are, a sinner, to the Lamb of God that taketh away the
sin of the world."

These words and the persuasion of this Swiss pastor helped
Charlotte to gain a deeper, more sincere grasp of the Christian salvation story. Apparently she saved these words, let
them season her soul, for it was almost fourteen years later
that she put down on paper:

> Just as I am, without one plea
> But that Thy blood was shed for me,
> And that Thou bidd'st me come to Thee,
> O Lamb of God, I come, I come!
>
> Just as I am, and waiting not
> To rid my soul of one dark blot,
> To Thee whose blood can cleanse each spot,
> O Lamb of God, I come, I come!
>
> Just as I am, though tossed about
> With many a conflict, many a doubt,
> Fightings and fears, within, without,
> O Lamb of God, I come, I come!
>
> Just as I am, poor, wretched, blind;
> Sight, riches, healing of the mind,
> Yea, all I need, in Thee I find,
> O Lamb of God, I come, I come!
>
> Just as I am, Thou wilt receive,

Wilt welcome, pardon, cleanse, relieve,
Because Thy promise I believe,
O Lamb of God, I come, I come!

Just as I am; Thy love unknown
Hath broken every barrier down;
Now to be Thine, yea, Thine alone,
O Lamb of God, I come, I come!

CHARLOTTE ELLIOTT

H. V. Elliott, the pastor-brother of Charlotte, once wrote,

> In the course of a long ministry, I hope I have
> been permitted to see some fruit of my labors, but
> I feel far more has been done by a single hymn of
> my sister's.

Miss Elliott was, however, not a one-hymn wonder. She composed more than a hundred and lived to see wide acceptance of her labors. Her faith and music touched a global chord. At her death more than a thousand letters were found, correspondence from people who expressed their personal appreciation for what "Just As I Am" had meant in their lives.

Fanny Crosby

Following the vast output of Wesley and Watts, a blind woman who lived to be ninety-five years of age wrote an amazing number of hymns used today in the Christian church. Fanny Crosby was afflicted with an eye ailment as an infant—and then suffered the wrong cure by a country doctor in upstate New York. At six weeks of age her sight was gone but most apparently, not her faith! By the time she was eight she would write:

> O what a happy soul am I
> Although I cannot see,
> I am resolved that in this world
> Contented I will be;
> How many blessings I enjoy
> That other people don't!

> To weep and sigh because I'm blind,
> I cannot, and I won't.

This gritty gal attended the New York Institute for the Blind for twelve years. During this time she became famous for her recitations before the Congress as well as various appearances at State legislatures. She later married a blind Methodist clergyman.

My own interest in Miss Crosby is her constant concern for the derelicts of urban society—which were close at hand during the years that she lived in Brooklyn, New York. For nearly a decade I was associated with the Bowery Mission in New York City, a rescue center that also appealed to Fanny during her active years in the same city.

In 1869 she wrote the words to, "Rescue the Perishing," a hymn inspired by one of her many visits to the mission. She had been commuting in a horse-drawn hack and put the words together on the way home. The Bowery remains to this day a place to:

> Rescue the perishing,
> Care for the dying;
> Snatch them in pity from sin and the grave;
> Weep o'er the erring one
> Lift up the fallen one,
> Tell them of Jesus the Mighty to save.

Miss Crosby had the unique skill of forming poems and hymns at spontaneous inspiration. She wrote several hymns for William H. Doane, another noted musician of the nineteenth century. In 1868 Doane played a tune for Fanny, wondering if she could provide the appropriate lyrics. He no sooner had finished his composition when she said, "Why, that's 'Safe in the Arms of Jesus.' " And indeed, it was.

> Safe in the arms of Jesus
> Safe on His gentle breast,
> There by His love o'ershaded,
> Sweetly my soul shall rest.

> Hark, 'tis the voice of angels,
> Borne in a song to me
> Over the fields of glory,
> Over the jasper sea.

No one really knows the grand total of hymns written by this blind composer. Some suggest at least 3,000, others say as high as 8,000. Whatever the total, Fanny Crosby wrote her way into musical history with songs such as: "All the Way My Saviour Leads Me," "Blessed Assurance, Jesus Is Mine," "I Am Thine, O Lord."

The enthusiasm of Fanny Crosby for her faith was shared by other women within the Christian church who turned their talents to writing hymns. Their zeal can be traced to the great revivals that swept Europe and America in the middle and late 1800s.

Several such American writers were Mary Lathbury, Anna Warner, Catherine Esling, Harriet Beecher Stowe, Phoebe Cary, and Elizabeth Prentiss. The frontier faith and the wide influence of revival theology (with its ordination of women) did not always set well with established music authorities. Gospel hymns were considered second-rate and their catchy tunes and clever rhythms were, to scholars such as David R. Breed, a sign of decadence in sacred song.

Decadent or delightful, they were nevertheless written, sung, and shared by thousands of ardent believers in the whole Christian community. Fanny Crosby advanced this mood by her tireless input into the musical bloodstream of the gospel movement. The Civil War and the westward development of the United States brought new ballads to a growing population. Fanny was asked by her music teacher, George Frederick Root, to provide the words for songs he had written. Swiftly came such popular lyrics as "Hazel Dell," "There's Music in the Air," and "Rosalie, the Prairie Flower."

One talent that Miss Crosby employed was the impulsive skill of reeling off verses at the sudden suggestion of the moment, a request by a friend, or the inspiration of some daily event. For anyone to write five or six thousand hymns, that skill would seem to be a prerequisite.

Isaac Watts too had this rhyming ability from early childhood. Once during family prayers, young Isaac burst out laughing. His father asked him the cause of this sudden outburst and Watts replied that he saw a mouse go up a bell-rope that hung next to the fireplace, and thus added this rhyme on the spot:

> A mouse for want of better stairs
> Ran up a rope to say his prayers.

This incessant rhyming of Watts and Crosby was not always appreciated by their families. Some considered it an ailment, surpassed only by the sickness of punning—which can be arrested but seldom cured.

Watts, like Crosby, had plenty of coaching from the family in this special skill. By age seven, Watts had already won medals for his rhymes and by twelve years of age he was spilling out verse in daily conversation as well as on paper. The irritation level got to his father, Deacon Enoch Watts, so much that he threatened to belt his son for this unending verse building. Isaac, bright and fearless replied, "O Father, do some pity take, and I will no more verses make!"

Although Fanny Crosby responded on several occasions to write secular verse, her great fame was established in the torrent of hymns that flowed from her brilliance. Clint Bonner in his *A Hymn Is Born* notes that Fanny faithfully followed certain patterns of prayer and preparation before writing and speaking. Whenever the blind poet spoke, she held a small testament in her hand. She said that it gave her strength for the task.

While writing verse she generally knelt in prayer for inspiration. One day she was very busy with other commitments and neglected her personal devotions. She felt unable to produce the material requested by her friend, William H. Doane. Then she immediately dropped to her knees in prayer and upon returning to her chair, promptly and without pause, dictated to her secretary, "Jesus Keep Me Near the Cross."

Bonner also reports the meeting between Fanny (known to many in later years as Aunt Fanny) and Phoebe Palmer (an evangelist's daughter and composer in her own right) who played a composition and requested some lyrics. She turned to discover Fanny on her knees right next to the piano. After this quiet interlude, she requested Miss Palmer to play the tune again and then dictated, without stopping:

> Blessed assurance, Jesus is mine!
> Oh, what a foretaste of glory divine!

Fanny Crosby expired writing hymns. She died on Lincoln's birthday (her favorite of the many presidents she had known). The day before her death a child in the neighborhood had died. During the evening, Fanny wrote this hymn at her bedside, wanting to give hope and support to her grief-stricken friends.

> You will reach the river brink
> Some sweet day, by and by
> You will find your broken link
> Some sweet day, by and by.
>
> O, the loved ones waiting there
> By the tree of life so fair,
> Till you come their joy to share
> Some sweet day, by and by.

The Popularity of the Gospel Song

Robert Guy McCutchan in his *Hymns in the Lives of Men* makes an essential comment about the popularity of the gospel song: its roots were in the catchy tunes of the Sunday school hymns that flooded America in the early and mid-1800s.

> The reason for stressing the influence of the Sunday school song or the gospel song should be

obvious: songs learned in childhood carry over
into adulthood . . . there was little difference (in
the 19th century) in the texts and tunes of the
Sunday school books and the gospel songs. Each
had a simple melody made easy to learn and recall
by its equally simple harmonization; there were
no rhythmic complications; and all were set to
texts in common, everyday English familiar to all.

Then McCutchan makes a keen appraisal of the abiding
power and influence of this simple music when he adds:

As the youngsters grew up and became leaders
in the churches, it was but natural they would
favor the kind of song with which they had long
been familiar, in many cases the only songs they
knew.

The gospel songs of the last century have endured, much
to the chagrin of some purists in music who consider them
sub-Christian or vulgar or both. The use of this music
brought a unity to diverse people opening up the frontiers
of America. It reflected poignantly on the hardships and
perils of day-to-day existence. Death and difficulty were constant companions.

Gospel hymns also were part of one's personal life bound-
aries which stabilized the events of daily life. The music was
from within, it was memorized and offered a support in difficult and threatening moments. Gospel songs were the working of a personal faith.

In a century without radio or television and on a frontier
without regular newspapers, frequent diversions of vaude-
ville, opera, or fairs, the experience of singing and learning
hymns was a vital channel of communication. The sharing
and reinforcing of values were deemed necessary and essential to the good life. The two constant themes of Christianity
of this century have been called "the joys of heaven and the
love of Christ" by McCutchan. Without this emphasis and

teaching, what did the frontier family have to hold soul and society together?

A prevailing force during this era was Philip Bliss. He became a revered figure in gospel music through his connection with Ira Sankey—and Sankey's association with the world-famous evangelist, Dwight L. Moody. Bliss was the first editor of *Gospel Hymns,* a popular volume of music used by Sankey. (Some experts maintain that Sankey's musical publications, printed from the 1870s and extended by the influence of Moody, exceeded more than 50 million copies.)

The Most Popular Gospel Hymns

When I was at the *Christian Herald,* hymn polls were taken regularly to judge the popularity of various hymns. Through the years (the *Herald* is nearly a century old) there have been three or four hymns that have always been in the top three: "The Old Rugged Cross," "In the Garden," and "Nearer My God to Thee." Others very close and always in the top ten are, "Rock of Ages," "Sweet Hour of Prayer," and "What a Friend We Have in Jesus."

"In the Garden" was written by C. Austin Miles in 1912. A native of Lakehurst, New Jersey, Miles gained recognition by playing the organ at age twelve in a Methodist church. Later in his life he was asked to write a hymn that "would be sympathetic in tone, breathing tenderness in every line, one that would bring hope to the hopeless, rest for the weary and downy pillows to dying beds." Miles apparently succeeded, for "In the Garden" is just that. Miles chose Mary Magdalene as the principal figure of his hymn, the Garden of the Resurrection as the place, and the love of Christ as the theme.

> I come to the garden alone,
>   While the dew is still on the roses,
> And the voice I hear, falling on my ear,
>   The Son of God discloses.

Chorus:
    And He walks with me, and He talks with me,
      And He tells me I am His own;
    And the joy we share as we tarry there,
      None other has ever known.

He speaks, and the sound of His Voice
    Is so sweet the birds hush their singing,
And the melody that He gave to me,
    Within my heart is ringing.

I'd stay in the garden with Him
    Tho' the night around me be falling,
But He bids me go; thro' the voice of woe
    His voice to me is calling.*
                C. AUSTIN MILES

"The Old Rugged Cross" is easily the most popular gospel hymn of this century. The hymn itself is as rugged as the old cross. It is carefully despised by most hymnologists and musicians—yet it survives. It may be too personal, too corny, too maudlin—or just too popular, for it is mentioned only briefly in a couple of the three dozen books that comprised the major references in the preparation of this book. It is one of the ironies of life, that the choice of the common people is ignored and snubbed by the experts. Written by George Bennard of Albion, Michigan, "The Old Rugged Cross" is a blend of Salvation Army and Methodist theology.

Cecil Northcott says matter-of-factly:

It is simple, evangelical theology and has all the accents of what John Wesley would call believers' believing! There are, of course, some superior people who despise the gospel-song type of hymn, but there is no mistaking the choice of the people . . .

Some years ago a scriptwriter for radio, and *Christian Herald* feature writer, Margaret Sangster, wrote:

I was in a radio studio the other night, listening to the broadcast of a program. Naturally I was interested. Interested in what the performers did and how they were handled and the precision with which the timing was accomplished. But the one thing that interested me more than the actual happenings in the studio, was something quite apart from the especial broadcast that was taking place. For, as I sat there, I was conscious of a great flurry going on in an outer office. I could see, as I sat there, a constant stream of messenger boys—and I was conscious of an equally constant answering of telephones. I couldn't help feeling that some great event was taking place—or was about to take place.

And so the moment that the broadcast was over, I went into that outer office and began to ask questions. "Why the excitement?" I asked of a pretty stenographer. "I've never seen such a bustling about." The girl smiled as she replied: "A very popular singer is going to broadcast tonight," she told me, "and people are sending in requests that he sing their favorite song. Curiously enough, with hardly an exception, it's the same song!"

"What song is it?" I asked. And I was both amazed and stirred to learn that the radio audience was asking for one of the splendid old revival hymns—"The Old Rugged Cross"!

> On a hill far away stood an old rugged cross,
> The emblem of suff'ring and shame;
> And I love that old cross where the dearest
>   and best
> For a world of lost sinners was slain.

Chorus:
> So I'll cherish the old rugged cross,
> Till my trophies at last I lay down;
> I will cling to the old rugged cross
> And exchange it some day for a crown.

Oh, that old rugged cross so despised by
the world,
Has a wondrous attraction for me;
For the dear Lamb of God left His glory
above,
To bear it to dark Calvary.

In the old rugged cross, stained with blood
so divine,
A wondrous beauty I see;
For 'twas on that old cross Jesus suffered
and died,
To pardon and sanctify me.

To the old rugged cross I will ever be true,
Its shame and reproach gladly bear;
Then He'll call me some day to my home far
away,
Where His glory forever I'll share.*

GEORGE BENNARD

A Song Born in Controversy

"Rock of Ages" continues to share the limelight in the popularity polls. In every known list, it is in the favored ten—often in the top five. The personal touch is present, the salvation story is clear and powerful, the lyrics easy to recall. Augustus Toplady created this hymn in 1775–1776. It was first published in *The Gospel Magazine*.

Toplady was originally attracted to the preaching of the Methodists. He was converted in his teens and advanced into manhood with some of the attitudes that emerged from childhood. He is quoted as writing in his journal at the tender age of eleven, "I am now arrived at the age of eleven years. I praise to God I can remember no dreadful crime; and not to me but to the Lord be the glory, Amen."

In his later theological development, Toplady was to turn against his early Methodist persuasion and embrace Calvinist teachings as being the truth of the gospel concerning salvation. He labeled Methodist Arminianism as false and John Wesley in even worse descriptions. The two Christian leaders struggled for years, with Toplady pouring out a flood of rancor, criticism, and libel in a whole series of sermons, pamphlets, letters, and printed materials. Wesley took the high road, rarely referring to his seething critic, noting, "I do not fight with chimney-sweeps."

Dr. Albert Bailey endorses Louis F. Benson's contention that all of the romance and apocryphal stories surrounding "Rock of Ages" are probably not correct. The most famous story is that of a large rock-like cave near the author's home, which offered protection during a sudden thunderstorm that threatened Toplady, that led to the song's inspiration. Another saga writer argues that during this protection from the elements, the author reached down to pick up a playing card and used this to write of his sheltering experience, not unlike the protection of God for his people. Bailey claims the dates are all wrong for such a supposition of the author being there.

Here it is important to read again the words:

> Rock of Ages, cleft for me,
> Let me hide myself in Thee!
> Let the water and the blood
> From Thy riven side which flowed,
> Be of sin the double cure,
> Cleanse me from its guilt and power.
>
> Not the labor of my hands
> Can fulfil Thy law's demands;
> Could my zeal no respite know,
> Could my tears forever flow,
> All for sin could not atone;
> Thou must save, and Thou alone.
>
> Nothing in my hand I bring;
> Simply to Thy cross I cling;
> Naked, come to Thee for dress;
> Helpless, look to Thee for grace;

Foul, I to the Fountain fly;
Wash me, Saviour, or I die.

While I draw this fleeting breath,
When my eyestrings break in death,
When I soar through tracts unknown,
See Thee on Thy judgment throne,—
Rock of Ages, cleft for me,
Let me hide myself in Thee!

In his authoritative work, *Studies in Familiar Hymns,* Dr. Benson suggests that Toplady really found the inspiration for the writing of this hymn from his great enemy and opponent in the faith, John Wesley. Toplady certainly was familiar with most of Wesley's printed material. Thirty years before the writing of "Rock," this material appeared in Wesley's *Hymn on the Lord's Supper.*

O Rock of Israel,
Rock of Salvation, Rock struck and cleft for me,
let those two Streams of blood and water which
once gushed out of Thy side, bring down Pardon
and Holiness into my soul. And let me thirst after
them now, as if I stood upon the Mountain whence
sprang this water; and near the Cleft of that Rock,
the wounds of my Lord, whence gushed this sacred
Blood.

Apparently in this same book, Hymn xxvii, there is an opening sentence which simply says: "Rock of Israel, cleft for me."

It may be that Toplady had a photographic memory that produced, decades later, the words for this hymn. It is difficult to believe that he would knowingly plagiarize his most detested opponent in the field of religion.

The important thing to remember in all this is that a fine song endured the rancor and jealousy that burned so incessantly in the soul of Toplady. Wesley is gone, Toplady long departed, but the words of "Rock of Ages" continue—apparently a product of both!

Revival Hymns of Historic Merit

"How Great Thou Art," one of the most popular contemporary hymns, came to us from Europe. This is the story of a hymn that was first a poem and became popular only through its present usage in North America—primarily the Billy Graham crusades and especially the singing of George Beverly Shea.

In 1885 Carl Boberg wrote his Swedish work, "O store Gud." Later in 1925 it was translated by Dr. Gustav Johnson when he was at North Park College. The message of the song is forceful and clear: God's power and majesty can be known personally by his children.

The history of this hymn is somewhat complicated. This song had been translated from Swedish into German, Russian, and Polish—as well as other Slavic dialects. Stuart K. Hine, a British missionary in the Ukraine discovered the hymn in Russia, was unaware of its Swedish origin, and attributed the lyrics to a Russian prisoner whom he believed to have written it in the early twenties.

In 1948 Hine produced an English adaptation of the Swedish hymn—which he attributed to the Russian source. All this simply proves the staying power of strong music and an even stronger theological commitment.

3

Singing the Destiny of a Nation

"'Tis not unlikely that this work of God's Spirit, that is so extraordinary and wonderful, it is the dawning, or at least a prelude, of that glorious work of God so often foretold in Scripture, which in the progress and issue of it shall renew the world of mankind . . . And there are many things that make it probable that this work will begin in America."

JONATHAN EDWARDS

Columbia, Columbia, to glory arise
The Queen of the world, and the child of the skies;
Thy genius commands thee; with rapture behold,
While ages on ages thy splendors unfold.

TIMOTHY DWIGHT

"In many minds the American was conceived as a new Adam in a new Eden, and the American nation as mankind's great second chance. Nothing better illustrates the continuity of this tradition than the patriotic hymns: 'America,' 'Battle Hymn of the Republic,' 'America the Beautiful.' "

from *A Religious History of the American People*

Civil War Songs

The emotion and fervor of the Civil War was caught up

in three intensely popular songs: "Dixie," "John Brown," and the "Battle Hymn of the Republic." The latter was the creative patriotic outburst of Julia Ward Howe who came to represent in music what Harriet Beecher Stowe created in her novel, *Uncle Tom's Cabin,* which depicted the sorrows and cruelties of slavery. More than a million people were to buy this book, but tens of millions were to sing "Mine eyes have seen the glory of the coming of the Lord."

Julia Ward Howe grew up in New York in the 1820s. Raised in the evangelical Ward family with Episcopal convictions, Julia became caught up in the liberal movement of her day and eventually married one of the leading humanitarians of that period, Dr. Samuel Gridley Howe. Dr. Howe was active in the anti-slavery movement and edited the abolitionist paper, *The Boston Commonwealth.* Julia pursued her progressive goals in the Bay area, was to become a staunch member of the Radical Club, and a steady reader of radical philosophy. Her religious persuasions took her into membership of the Church of the Disciples in Boston, and into close relationship with its pastor, Dr. James Freeman Clarke.

It was with Reverend Clarke that in the fall of 1861 Mrs. Howe visited Washington, D.C., where she was a guest of President Lincoln. Riding through the adjacent army camps they heard so many soldiers singing "John Brown's Body." (She once received Brown in her Boston home.) Dismayed at the poor selection of words to the song, Julia Howe returned that evening to the Willard Hotel in the capital and wrote out her own lyrics, "The Battle Hymn of the Republic":

> Mine eyes have seen the glory
>   of the coming of the Lord;
> He is trampling out the vintage
>   where the grapes of wrath are stored;
> He hath loosed the fateful lightning
>   of His terrible swift sword;
>   His truth is marching on.

I have seen Him in the watch-fires
    of a hundred circling camps,
They have builded Him an altar
    in the evening dews and damps;
I can read His righteous sentence
    by the dim and flaring lamps.
      His day is marching on.

I have read a fiery gospel
    writ in burnished rows of steel;
"As ye deal with my contemner,
    so with you my grace shall deal";
Let the Hero, born of woman,
    crush the serpent with His heel,
      Since God is marching on.

He hath sounded forth the trumpet
    that shall never call retreat;
He is sifting out the hearts of men
    before His judgment seat;
Oh, be swift, my soul, to answer Him!
    be jubilant, my feet!
      Our God is marching on.

In the beauty of the lilies
    Christ was born across the sea,
With a glory in His bosom
    that transfigures you and me;
As He died to make men holy,
    let us die to make men free,
      While God is marching on.
         JULIA WARD HOWE

In the book *Stories of Great National Songs* Nicholas Smith reveals some of the mood which surrounded the Civil War year of 1861:

> This need of a new national hymn to meet new and exciting conditions, one that would be the great peace song, yet the war song of the nation— the national heart-beat set to music—was deeply

felt at the very beginning of the civil war. At the
request of many prominent Union men, a committee, composed of scholars and statesmen, among
whom were George William Curtis, Hamilton
Fish, and General John A. Dix, was appointed to
select such a hymn for the use of the homes in the
North and the army in the field. The committee
waited three months for such a song. Twelve hundred competitors presented their compositions for
the prize of $250 for the words and $250 for the
music; but not one of them was accepted. The
committee found that there was no soul-feeling, no
fire of patriotism, running through any of the
songs.

Colonel Smith (as he liked to be addressed) researched
some of the difficulties faced by Julia Ward Howe. One was
the put-down attitude of James Russell Lowell, long-time
editor of the *Atlantic Monthly*. At an earlier period he refused to publish a piece by Mrs. Howe, stating belligerently
that "no woman can write a poem" and citing Mrs. Browning
as a "conspicuous illustration of this fact!" Lowell was succeeded at the *Atlantic* by James T. Fields who took a different view of Mrs. Howe's works, paid her $5.00 for the "Battle
Hymn of the Republic" and even helped her in his suggestions for a title. Yet when this poem was published, her name
was not mentioned or credited in the table of contents.

Florence Howe Hall has written concerning this national
hymn:

> The soul of the vast army of the American peo-
> ple, struggling for utterance in the greatest crisis
> of its existence, at last found a voice to express its
> meaning, and its aspiration—the voice of a woman.

Of historic interest is the fact that both popular songs of
the Civil War, the "Battle Hymn of the Republic" and
"Dixie," have survived to be cherished in all sections of the
nation. "Dixie" was written by Daniel D. Emmett in New

York, who was a member of Bryant's Minstrels in 1859. As the Howe hymn became favored in the South, so did "Dixie" in the North, where it was sung to Republican words in the campaign of 1860. Soon after the southern surrender at Appomattox Lincoln requested the army band to play "Dixie," after remarking, "as we captured the Confederate army, we have also captured the Confederate tune and both belong to us."

The original tune had been composed by a southerner, John W. Staffe of Richmond, Virginia. It eventually was published in the *Atlantic Monthly* and became the marching song of the Union army. Julia Ward Howe was recognized as a leader in women's suffrage and international peace. Before her death in 1910, she received the Doctor of Laws degree at Smith College and had authored several books.

The music of the Civil War—both secular and religious—demonstrates some of the blends, overlays, and combinations that surge through this country when faith and patriotism are linked. As Gilbert Chase has proposed

> If anyone doubts that these revival songs are woven deep in the fabric of America's music, deep in the strands of our national culture, let him recall a song that all Americans know, that they have sung for generations, and that each rising generation inherits anew—the song that we know as "The Battle Hymn of the Republic."

Dr. Chase goes on to remind us that this hymn was once "a rousing camp-meeting spiritual, with a typical repetitive stanza and a singing hallelujah chorus."

The brooding over the War between the States began long before the first shots were exchanged at Harpers Ferry. The anxiety and moral sensitivity to the slavery question had stirred many Americans both North and South. Such a powerful and ageless institution may have seemed solid as concrete to the masses, but to a probing minority, it could not forever stand. One such visionary was James Russell Lowell whose

life (1819–1891) closely parallels Julia Ward Howe in sentiment as well as place—Boston. Before writing "Once to
Every Man and Nation" (1844), Lowell had tried his hand at
law, having graduated from Harvard with two degrees and
much interest in the subject. His attempt at law failed and
his zeal for writing was apparent to himself and the public.
By 1855 he was so widely acclaimed as author and poet that
Harvard granted him the Chair of Modern Language and
Literature, succeeding no less a personality than Henry Wads-
worth Longfellow. Later, Lowell was to be in diplomatic
service to Spain and Great Britain. Honors poured in from
Oxford, Cambridge, Harvard, St. Andrews, Edinburgh, every-
where and at last from the American Hall of Fame in 1905.
Yet Lowell is best known to us in "Once to Every Man and
Nation."

> Once to every man and nation
>   Comes the moment to decide,
> In the strife of truth with false-hood,
>   For the good or evil side;
> Some great cause, God's new Messiah,
>   Offering each the bloom or blight,
> And the choice goes by forever
>   'Twixt that darkness and that light.
>
> By the light of burning martyrs,
>   Jesus' bleeding feet I track,
> Toiling up new Calvaries ever
>   With the cross that turns not back;
> New Occasions teach new duties,
>   Time makes ancient good uncouth;
> They must upward still and onward,
>   Who would keep abreast of truth.
>
> Though the cause of evil prosper,
>   Yet 'tis truth alone is strong;
> Though per portion be the scaffold,
>   And upon the throne be wrong,
> Yet that scaffold sways the future,
>   And, behind the dim unknown,

Standeth God within the shadow,
Keeping watch above His own.
JAMES RUSSELL LOWELL

Here powerful biblical passages and symbols are aligned in
the struggle with slavery and the ultimate providence of God
to realize justice in the life of his people.

It appears that we are not sentimentally moved to write
hymns of affection and love to our native land. Patriotism
has taken many turns in the past decades, and one of them
is the embarrassed and awkward feelings that some people
have in openly expressing patriotism—so much so that few
write poems of praise to their country and fewer yet write
hymns of support and honor. This certainly was not true in
the nineteenth century. Fresh from the events of the American Revolution, many artists and composers were deeply com-
mitted to the cause of the colonies.

In 1832 a young theological student at Andover Newton
Seminary in Massachusetts was invited by Lowell Mason to
translate some hymns from the German books he had received from Europe. As Samuel Francis Smith pored over the
volumes, looking for something suitable for children's use,
he was taken with the tune "God Save the King"—a British
melody in a German publication—one that was unfamiliar
to him at that time. Smith later remarked:

> I instantly felt the impulse to write a patriotic
> hymn of my own adapted to the tune. Picking up
> a scrap of waste paper which lay near me, I wrote
> at once, probably within half an hour, the hymn
> "America" as it is now known everywhere.

The popularity of this hymn was immediate. It was first
sung in the Park Street Church in Boston on July 4, 1832,
and under the leadership of Lowell Mason, then at the height
of his career.

Presently there are those who feel that it is no longer able
to qualify as a national anthem, being more a regional hymn
with its special references to the "woods and templed hills"

of New England. Albert Edward Bailey feels that "patriotism and religion are indistinguishably blended" in this work. Smith was a scholar of the first order. He knew and read a dozen languages well and became famous, however, for this one song that took less than a half hour to compose.

My country, 'tis of thee,
Sweet land of liberty,
    Of thee I sing;
Land where my fathers died,
Land of the pilgrims' pride,
From every mountain side
    Let freedom ring.

My native country,—thee,
Land of the noble free,—
    Thy name I love;
I love they rocks and rills,
Thy woods and templed hills;
My heart with rapture thrills
    Like that above.

Let music swell the breeze,
And ring from all the trees
    Sweet freedom's song:
Let mortal tongues awake;
Let all that breathe partake;
Let rocks their silence break,
    The sound prolong.

Our fathers' God, to Thee,
Author of liberty,
    To Thee we sing;
Long may our land be bright
With freedom's holy light;
Protect us by Thy might,
    Great God, our King.

SAMUEL FRANCIS SMITH

Much of the music of our patriotic hymns comes out of the nineteenth century—a time of testing and recommitment for millions of Americans. The War between the States had generated a great deal of singing to go along with the fervor and faith that this conflict unearthed. The year 1876 also marked the first one hundred years for the young nation and not a little effort was put out to mark the Centennial. Philadelphia had an enormous show—built to exceed any observation in modern history. The Centennial Exposition, as it was called, spread out over nearly 300 acres. The principal structure cost four and a half million dollars. The total underwriting of the seven-month national birthday party (which more than 9 million people attended) aside from Congressional, state, and city grants exceeded ten million dollars. It was some party! And it was a wild year too. The Sioux Indians ignored all the pretentious claims of the United States and slaughtered General Custer and 261 men of the Seventh Cavalry at the Little Big Horn River. Alexander Graham Bell patented his telephone and Mark Twain gave the world *The Adventures of Tom Sawyer*.

There was a lot of both good and bad music around. The musical director for the whole effort at the Exposition was a noted conductor, Theodore Thomas, who confessed that the expenses wiped out his personal fortune and took a dozen years to settle. The prominent German composer, Richard Wagner, composed an opening day number—which totally depressed and angered Mr. Thomas. Whittier's "Centennial Hymn" (music by John Knowles Paine) was heard the same day.

While all the excitement and clamor were taking place in Philadelphia, an Episcopal pastor wrote "God of Our Fathers" for the people of Brandon, Vermont, and their celebration on July 4, 1876. Although it was not in print for another dozen years, it slowly and steadily gained wide acceptance as being an important part of national celebrations. The Reverend Daniel Crane Roberts spent nearly his entire ministerial career in New England. He held congregational posts in Lowell, Massachusetts, Montpelier and Brandon, Vermont, and in his closing years was head of St. Paul's

Academy in Concord, New Hampshire. Although not located in the great plan of celebrations and observances that attracted millions to Philadelphia, Roberts's hymn did find a lasting niche in American history and singing.

> God, of our fathers, whose almighty hand
> Leads forth in beauty all the starry band
> Of shining worlds in splendor through the skies,
> Our grateful songs before Thy throne arise.
>
> Thy love divine hath led us in the past;
> In this free land by Thee our lot is cast;
> Be Thou our Ruler, Guardian, Guide, and Stay;
> Thy word our law, Thy paths our chosen way.
>
> From war's alarms, from deadly pestilence,
> Be Thy strong arm our ever sure defense;
> Thy true religion in our hearts increase,
> Thy bounteous goodness nourish us in peace.
>
> Refresh Thy people on their toilsome way,
> Lead us from night to never-ending day;
> Fill all our lives with love and grace divine,
> And glory, laud, and praise be ever Thine.
>   DANIEL CRANE ROBERTS

One of the great all-encompassing national songs is "America the Beautiful." In this hymn we have the expression of an eastern author observing the creativity of man (at the Alabaster City of the Chicago Exposition in 1893) and then the vast grandeur of the universe in the soaring heights of the Rockies (at Pike's Peak) and the sweeping beauty of prairie and plain.

Katharine Lee Bates was another New Englander from Boston who took seriously the notions of the Christian faith and was uninhibited about putting it down on paper for others to share and sing. She once wrote of her trip West, with its first stop in booming, boasting Chicago:

> The White City made such a strong appeal to
> patriotic feeling that it was in no small degree

responsible for at least the last stanza of "America the Beautiful."

It was with this quickened and deepened sense of America that we went on—my New England eyes delighting in the wind-waved gold of the vast wheat fields.

And then came the mountains. They were purple and they still are purple in late evening, with the approach of twilight.

> O beautiful for spacious skies,
>   For amber waves of grain,
> For purple mountain majesties
>   Above the fruited plain!
>   America! America!
>   God shed His grace on thee
> And crown thy good with brotherhood
>   From sea to shining sea!
>
> O beautiful for pilgrim feet,
>   Whose stern, impassioned stress
> A thoroughfare for freedom beat
>   Across the wilderness!
>   America! America!
>   God mend thine every flaw,
> Confirm thy soul in self-control,
>   Thy liberty in law!
>
> O beautiful for heroes proved
>   In liberating strife,
> Who more than self their country loved,
>   And mercy more than life!
>   America! America!
>   May God thy gold refine,
> Till all success be nobleness,
>   And every gain divine!
>
> O beautiful for patriot dream
>   That sees beyond the years
> Thine alabaster cities gleam
>   Undimmed by human tears!
>   America! America!

God shed His grace on thee

And crown thy good with brotherhood

From sea to shining sea!

KATHARINE LEE BATES

In his early writings, Sinclair Lewis recalled the celebration of July 4, 1902, with his friend, Fisher. They walked out of town, Sauk Centre, Minnesota, and reached Long Point, on Fairy Lake. Here they:

> took some lunch and some books . . . after lunch I read the Declaration of Independence and Fisher, the Constitution of the United States. That was all of our "celebration" yet me thinks it was no less acceptable to the great Author of Independence than are the fire-works, toy cannons, horse races, potato races, fat-men's races, baseball games, lemonade stand, merry-go-rounds, etc., etc. of the celebrations of others. . . .

It was this affection for country, the high loyalty to the founding of the nation, and the words themselves that appealed to these young men in their journey toward manhood. Katharine Bates caught a large portion of the sentiment that pervaded American life and surfaced so explicitly in the remarks of Lewis.

Another thoughtful hymnist of the middle nineteenth century was Dr. Robert Lowry of Brooklyn, New York. A Baptist preacher, Lowry wrote "Shall We Gather at the River" during the height of an epidemic in the summer of 1864. Hundreds of people were struck down during this pestilence and Lowry heard the question asked by a dying patient, "Pastor, we have parted at the river of death; shall we meet again at the river of life?" This question haunted the writer until he gathered the words and music to respond:

Shall we gather at the river,

Where bright angel-feet have trod,

With its crystal tide forever

Flowing by the throne of God?

Chorus:
>Yes, we'll gather at the river,
>>The beautiful, the beautiful river;
>Gather with the saints at the river
>>That flows by the throne of God.

On the margin of the river,
>Washing up its silver spray,
We will walk and worship ever
>All the happy, golden day.

Ere we reach the shining river,
>Lay we every burden down:
Grace our spirits will deliver,
>And provide a robe and crown.

At the smiling of the river,
>Mirror of the Saviour's face,
Saints, whom death will never sever,
>Lift their songs of saving grace.

Soon we'll reach the silver river;
>Soon our pilgrimage will cease;
Soon our happy hearts will quiver
>With the melody of peace.
>>ROBERT LOWRY

Lowry continued to be a person of note both in the pulpit and in publishing. He edited at least a dozen hymnbooks before his death in 1899.

Yet it was a source of irritation to him that his songs seemed for destiny while his preaching accompanied him to the grave. He often argued that his hymns were really an avocation—it was the gospel message of his preaching that he coveted for people. He wrote "Where Is My Wandering Boy Tonight?" for the temperance movement of 1877. Lowry remained in Brooklyn until 1876 when he was appointed professor at Bucknell University. Here he stayed for six years, and then finally completed his ministry in Plainfield, New Jersey.

In the 1870s, a young singing evangelist, Savilla Kring,

first sang "I'm a Child of the King" at Chautauqua, New York. This young woman had a voice which stirred audiences and she was to become the first ordained woman in the Evangelical Church. As part of an evangelistic quartet, she became famous on the camp meeting circuit which included Old Orchard, Maine; Round Lake, New York; and Ocean Grove, New Jersey.

It was in Ocean Grove, where on a summer Sunday morning in 1881 she dedicated the new pavilion. A few miles away lay President James A. Garfield, mortally wounded by an assassin's bullet which struck him as he boarded a train in Washington, D.C. Taken to his home in Elberon, near Long Branch, New Jersey, the failing chief executive heard Savilla Kring sing with her golden voice:

> My Father is rich in houses and lands,
> He holdeth the wealth of the world in His hand!
> Of rubies and diamonds, of silver and gold,
> His coffers are full, He has riches untold.
>
> My Father's own Son, the Saviour of men,
> Once wandered on earth as the poorest of them.
> But now He is pleading our pardon on high,
> That we may be His when He comes by and by.
>
> I once was an outcast stranger on earth,
> A sinner by choice, and alien by birth;
> But I've been adopted, my name's written down,
> An heir to a mansion, a robe and a crown.
>
> A tent or a cottage why should I care?
> They're building a palace for me over there;
> Tho' exiled from home, yet, still I may sing:
> All Glory to God, I'm a child of the King.

> Chorus:
> I'm a child of the King, A child of the King:
> With Jesus my Saviour I'm a child of the King.

"I'm a Child of the King" became a favorite parlor hymn in my family's musical life. Savilla Kring was my grandmother and her loyalty to music, to singing gospel hymns, was essential to the broadening of our faith (and also for a good understanding of the meaning of ordination for women). Almost every Christian family has some favorite songs and hymns, some special gospel notes which link the past and the present, which have the power to remind and recall that which is worthy of our contemporary attention. Religious music keeps rolling on. Yet is it not a cumulative experience or how else would we understand so much that is incorporated in our collective memory of being Americans?

Much of that memory is the shared beginnings in music that was sung at school and church. The new piety that swept America in the wake of the great evangelistic crusades of the nineteenth century was clinched by the songs of that time. Sydney Ahlstrom in his *Religious History of the American People* suggests that, "What a Friend We Have in Jesus" (1868), "Jesus Keep Me Near the Cross" (1869), "Blessed Assurance, Jesus Is Mine" (1873), "Softly and Tenderly Jesus Is Calling" (1909), "I Come to the Garden Alone" (1912) were the songs that "heard once, they would be remembered forever. Few ties were there that bound American Protestants so firmly together in a common popular tradition."

Ahlstrom illustrates this expression by recalling a Broadway musical, *Say Darling* (1958), which contained a scene where several hard-boiled theatrical producers are holding some auditions for their play. The script they are working with requires the singing of a revival hymn, "Let the Lower Lights Be Burning." Suddenly their midwestern, Protestant roots surface as they all join in singing every stanza as well as the refrain.

> Brightly beams our Father's mercy
> From His lighthouse evermore,
> But to us He gives the keeping
> Of the lights along the shore.
>
> Dark the night of sin has settled,

Loud the angry billows roar;
Eager eyes are watching, longing,
For the lights along the shore.

Trim your feeble lamp, my brother:
Some poor sailor tempest tossed,
Trying now to make the harbor,
In the darkness may be lost.

Chorus:
Let the lower lights be burning!
Send a gleam across the wave!

PHILIP PAUL BLISS

"Brightly Beams Our Father's Mercy" (Lower Lights) was the work of a talented musician Philip Paul Bliss of Rome, Pennsylvania. At the age of twenty-six he went to Chicago where he was successfully employed by the Root and Cady Music House. Much of his material was prepared for church schools and evangelical services. Bliss was gifted with a fine voice and had an exceptional talent for creating new tunes for Christian leaders.

Bliss was a follower of Dwight L. Moody and returned home inspired by one of the evangelist's illustrations to write this particular hymn. Moody, in graphic and convincing language, had told the story of a captain guiding his ship into the Cleveland harbor. It was a bleak and stormy night and the lighthouse was operating only one light. The captain was heard to shout, "Where are the lower lights?"

"They have gone out, Sir," was the reply.

"Can we make the harbor?"

"We must or we perish," was the last reply.

With great drama, Moody described the crashing and sinking of the ship as it struck the unlighted rocky coast.

From this he went on to exclaim, "The Master will take care of the great lighthouse; let us keep the lower lights burning."

Bliss was really taken by this illustration and the hymn

lyrics and words were quickly written at home. He also wrote "Almost Persuaded" in 1871:

> "Almost persuaded," now to believe;
> "Almost persuaded," Christ to receive;
>   Seems now some soul to say,
>   "Go, Spirit, go Thy way,
>   Some more convenient day,
>   On Thee I'll call."

> "Almost persuaded," come, come today;
> "Almost persuaded," turn not away;
>   Jesus invites you here,
>   Angels are ling'ring near
>   Prayers rise from hearts so dear,
>   O wand'rer, come.

> "Almost persuaded," harvest is past!
> "Almost persuaded," doom comes at last!
>   "Almost" cannot avail;
>   "Almost" is but to fail!
>   Sad, sad, that bitter wail,
>   "Almost" but lost!

English Hymns

Just as the gospel hymns of nineteenth-century piety made for long and significant changes within the church and the homes of its members, so had the alterations begun in the Church of England when people like Reginald Heber had a deep dissatisfaction with the singing styles of the English. Heber was one of the bright, talented young Christians to enter the church, first as a local parish priest, then as a missionary bishop in India. He was one hymn writer who could turn out music for the right liturgical occasion and discover that his works endured far beyond the moment. "Holy, Holy, Holy" was prepared for Trinity Sunday—the Sunday which follows Easter by eight weeks. The lesson usually read is from John 3. The emphasis is to proclaim the meaning and centrality of the Father, Son, and Holy

Spirit in the life of the worshipers. Heber wrote this hymn in 1827 at the request of his father-in-law who wanted a new song to give the people, "something for them to sing in the morning." According to valid reports, Heber wrote the words in five or six minutes and the tune is usually the one by Dykes.

Heber wrote other hymns which reflect the desire for missionary service, a calling which he was able to fulfill by going to India. "From Greenland's Icy Mountains," "Brightest and Best of the Sons of the Morning," as well as "By Cool Siloam's Shady Rill" were among those written when Heber was an English country parson.

Of "Holy, Holy, Holy" Albert Bailey has a thoughtful summary:

> No hymn has greater dignity and uplifting power; none is more thoroughly liturgical, fit to be sung by vast multitudes in grand cathedrals, while the organ rolls its thrilling thunders . . . the hymn consists almost entirely of ephithets—words that seek to define the nature of the God we worship. He is Lord, God the Almighty, the Holy, merciful mighty, the one who was and is and is to come . . . this hymn of Heber's satisfies the needs of the Church universal. . . .

Heber died in 1826, a short three years after his arrival in India. Much of his work was not published until after his death, such was the caution within the Church of England.

One hymn of enduring beauty and written in the awareness that life was drawing to a close is, "Abide with Me." It was written by Henry Francis Lyte, an Anglican clergyman who spent most of his ministry in Brixham, England. Lyte was never in good health and in his later years would winter on the French Riviera, returning to his beloved parish for the summer and fall season. He was a great organizer and gathered a church school of some eight hundred children. As one historian exclaimed, Lyte created "hymns for his little ones, hymns for his hardy fishermen, and hymns for sufferers like himself." "Abide with Me" was surely for himself as well as for his flock. It nearly did not get written. In 1847 he went to the seaside near his village one evening and wrote the words, completing them for his family that night. Two months later he died and was buried in an English cemetery near the Mediterranean.

"Abide with Me" is really a poem of preparation for death. It also has wide popularity with the well as with the ailing because it touches a universal concern with great hope and assurance.

> Abide with me! fast falls the eventide;
> The darkness deepens; Lord, with me abide!
> When other helpers fail, and comforts flee,
> Help of the helpless, O abide with me!
>
> Swift to its close ebbs out life's little day;
> Earth's joys grow dim, its glories pass away;
> Change and decay in all around I see;
> O Thou who changest not, abide with me!
>
> I need Thy presence every passing hour:
> What but Thy grace can foil the tempter's power?
> Who like Thyself my guide and stay can be?
> Through cloud and sunshine, O abide with me!
>
> I fear no foe, with Thee at hand to bless:
> Ills have no weight, and tears no bitterness.
> Where is death's sting? where, grave, thy victory?
> I triumph still, if Thou abide with me!
>
> Hold Thou Thy cross before my closing eyes,
> Shine through the gloom, and point me to the
>   skies;
> Heaven's morning breaks, and earth's vain shadows
>   flee;
> In life, in death, O Lord, abide with me!
>   HENRY FRANCIS LYTE

Navy Hymn

Through the years most Americans have had a vague knowledge of the "Navy Hymn." But following the assassination and the funeral for the late President John F. Kennedy, this music became deeply entwined in the lives of millions of people. It is the official anthem of the United States Naval Academy and appears in some hymnbooks as well.

Like many of our hymns, it has a British beginning. Entitled, "Eternal Father," it was written by William Whiting who headed the famous Winchester College Choristers' School. He was Anglican by religious tradition and wrote this seafaring song in 1860:

Eternal Father, strong to save,
Whose arm doth bind the restless wave,
Who bidd'st the mighty ocean deep
Its own appointed limits keep:
O hear us when we cry to Thee
For those in peril on the sea.

O Saviour, whose almighty word
The winds and waves submissive heard,
Who walkedst on the foaming deep
And calm amid its rage didst sleep:
O hear us when we cry to Thee
For those in peril on the sea.

O sacred Spirit, who didst brood
Upon the chaos dark and rude,
Who bad'st its angry tumult cease,
And gavest light and life and peace:
O hear us when we cry to Thee
For those in peril on the sea.

O Trinity of love and power,
Our brethren shield in danger's hour;
From rock and tempest, fire and foe,
Protect them wher-so-e'er they go;
And ever let there rise to Thee
Glad hymns of praise from land and sea.
                              WILLIAM WHITING

Dr. Albert Edward Bailey in his *The Gospel in Hymns* notes the clear reference of the text to Psalm 107:23–32 as well as the stanzas arranged to coincide with Father, Son, and Holy Spirit. In a personal reflection, Dr. Bailey states that he crossed the Atlantic forty-nine times and this hymn was sung at Morning Prayer every Sunday "that we were at sea under the British flag." Americans have long been out from under the British crown, yet forever linked in spirit by the words and music of this lovely song of the sea.

Another song linked to the ocean is "Nearer My God to Thee." It was written by the English author, Sarah F. Adams, in 1841. She is credited with hundreds of hymns, but "Nearer My God to Thee" achieved world fame through its association with the sinking of the *Titanic* on April 14, 1912. At its sailing from Southampton, England, bound for New York, the White Star liner, *Titanic* was considered to be one of the great ships of the world. It was built at a cost exceeding seven million dollars. It carried more than 2,000 passengers and crew. During the night it struck an iceberg off New-foundland and carried 1,517 people to the bottom of the ocean. Seven hundred passengers were rescued. What remains in the memory of our civilization is the orchestra playing "Nearer My God to Thee" in the final hours of the ship's sinking. At times the passengers on deck, unable to reach the lifeboats and aware that life belts were in short supply, joined in the singing of this classic hymn.

> Nearer, my God, to Thee!
>   Nearer to Thee!
> E'en though it be a cross
>   That raiseth me,
> Still all my song shall be,
> Nearer, my God, to Thee,
>   Nearer to Thee!
>
> Though, like the wanderer,
>   The sun gone down,
> Darkness be over me,
>   My rest a stone,
> Yet in my dreams I'd be

Nearer, my God, to Thee,
  Nearer to Thee!

There let my way appear
  Steps unto heaven;
All that Thou sendest me
  In mercy given;
Angels to beckon me
Nearer, my God, to Thee,
  Nearer to Thee!

Then with my waking thoughts,
  Bright with Thy praise,
Out of my stony griefs
  Bethel I'll raise,
So by my woes to be
Nearer, my God, to Thee,
  Nearer to Thee!

Or if on joyful wing,
  Cleaving the sky,
Sun, moon, and stars forgot,
  Upwards I fly;
Still all my song shall be,
Nearer, my God, to Thee,
  Nearer to Thee!
                    SARAH ADAMS

Before his death, President McKinley requested that this song be sung at his funeral. The martyred president established the song everywhere in America—as well as overseas. King Edward asked that it be played for the memorial service held in McKinley's honor in Westminster Abbey. It was for James Freeman Clarke, in 1844, to introduce this hymn to America and with it a fine tune prepared by Lowell Mason in 1856 that clinched its popular use in the United States. Amos Wells recalls that it was sung at the Boston Peace Jubilee in 1872, "by nearly fifty thousand voices and the venerable composer himself in the audience." Other vivid references in American history cite the Johnstown flood in 1889 when a railroad train plunged into the waters, entrapping hundreds of people. The persons aboard were reported to have sung this hymn before the cars finally collapsed in the torrent. It has been translated into many languages and is a favorite of Christians around the world.

Some Surprises

Most singing groups enjoy "Onward, Christian Soldiers" and almost every church school in the world teaches this popular hymn to its children and youth. It has a stirring melody to accompany the vivid and easily remembered lyrics. Fortunately, the history of the hymn is as exciting and inspirational as the composition itself.

Sabine Baring-Gould was a high church Anglican priest who served the coal mining community of Horbury, England. As curate of this bleak, worn industrial town on the edge of nowhere, he took a keen interest in the children and youth of the area. He began his teaching ministry on the upper and lower floors of a building which also housed the local post office. Out of this unlikely flop house he fashioned a chapel and rooms for Sunday school.

Baring-Gould wrote "Onward, Christian Soldiers" in 1865. A year earlier he graduated from Cambridge following extensive studies in Europe. The thought behind this hymn and the inspiration for its writing, he tells in his own words:

> It was written in a very simple fashion, without a thought for publication. Whitmonday is a great day for school festivals in Yorkshire, and one Whitmonday it was arranged that our school should join its forces with that of a neighboring village. I wanted the children to sing when marching from one village to the other, but couldn't think of anything quite suitable, so I sat up at night resolved to write something myself. "Onward, Christian Soldiers" was the result. It was written in great haste [less than fifteen minutes, it is said]. Certainly nothing has surprised me more than its popularity.

Baring-Gould went on to other parishes as well as a broadened writing ministry. In his ninety years (1834–1924) he affected countless people with the unending flow of published materials—totalling some eighty books—in many fields: from theology and sermons, to travel and fiction. Baring-Gould was a bright, brilliant, loving person who eventually inherited the family estate in north Devon—providing him with economic stability and a wide variety of posts to which he assigned himself: justice of the peace and rector of the local parish which surrounded his manor.

The life of Baring-Gould merits a full length film because of its romance, excitement, and creativity. He once saved a young woman from drowning in the Calder River—a Miss Grace Taylor who worked in one of the factories near his Horbury chapel. Baring-Gould became attracted to this young lady, a romance developed between them, and he ended up paying for her education, marrying her a year later with a classic honeymoon in Switzerland. One can see how Charles Dickens found so much of his material in the drama of people around him.

"Onward, Christian Soldiers" is headed for its second century of popular acceptance. Baring-Gould did not write it as a war song but directed its words and emphasis to the imaginary battles of children—which unfortunately have a way of becoming real in the worldly conflicts of adults. The hymn has marked important historic events, such as those described by Cecil Northcott in *Hymns We Love*. Northcott identifies that summer morning at sea, when in August, 1941, the British battleship, *Prince of Wales,* was hosting the Atlantic conference between Winston Churchill and Franklin Roosevelt. The American president and the British prime minister were trying to reach essential agreements on their dealing with the Axis powers in World War II. The Atlantic Charter was signed at this meeting and one memorable worship service was held with the sailors of both fleets and the heads of state sharing in the public praise of God.

Each leader was asked to select hymns to be used in the

joint service. President Roosevelt, close personally to the
U.S. Navy, asked for "Eternal Father, Strong to Save," the
Navy hymn. Churchill requested two songs: "Our God, Our
Help in Ages Past" and "Onward, Christian Soldiers." Dr.
Northcott remembers that when Churchill returned home
he broadcasted this message to the British empire:

> We sang "Onward, Christian Soldiers" and indeed,
> I felt that this was no vain presumption but that
> we had the right to feel that we were serving a
> cause for the sake of which a trumpet has sounded
> from on high. When I looked upon that densely
> packed congregation of fighting men of the same
> language, of the same faith, of the same funda-
> mental laws, of the same ideals . . . it swept across
> me that here was the only hope, but also the sure
> hope, of saving the world from measureless degra-
> dation.
>
> from BBC

4

Singing the Harmony of Our Differences

"Meanwhile, about 4,000 people had crowded into the church. In one gallery were a 200 voice choir and an orchestra with over 100 guitars, violins, and mandolins. The singing began in stepped-up rhythm, and soon the whole church was pulsing with vitality. As the singing progressed religious dancing appeared. On all faces were intense, rapt expressions; obviously, the people were lost in religious emotion." *

ALAN WALKER

"Superior melody results from the same recipe, with the difference that certain ingredients are blessed with the distortion of Genius."

NED ROREM
American composer

"For nothing dies, said the People. The body which has been lent to us for the time we are here goes back into our mother the earth. The spirit goes back also into the land of peace and summer from which it came. Even the thought

* Alan Walker, "Where Pentecostalism Is Mushrooming," in *The Christian Century*, January 17, 1968.

83

which has been put into the making of the beads and the jewels and the clothing we wear goes back. For the thought comes from the Great Spirit and is to be treasured." (And they chanted:)

> Now you go on your way alone
> What you now are, we know not;
> To what clan you now belong, we know not;
> From now on, you are not of this earth.
> > from *Traders to the Navajos*
> > The Wetherills of Kayenta

Music from Other Traditions

SHAKERS

Members of the most interesting sect to develop a distinct style of religious music—and dance—were called Shakers. Coming from England, they were first known as The Society of Believers in Christ's Second Appearing. These devout and determined Christians did not gain much of a following until a major revival hit New Lebanon, New York—not far from the Massachusetts border. The Shakers, an offshoot of the more familiar Quaker communities, had purchased some farm land and were following their principles of belief and action under the guidance of John Hocknell, Ann Lee (whom many believed to have talked with the risen Lord and proclaimed his imminent second coming), and her chief apostle, James Whitaker.

The era of the Great Awakening and the specific impulse from the Baptist revivals held in this district brought inquirers and followers to the initial Shaker commune around 1870. According to Edward D. Andrews, in their search for salvation, these new converts found:

> A fellowship literally following the example of the primitive apostolic church: men and women living together in celibate purity, holding all goods in common, working industriously with their hands, speaking and singing in unknown tongues, worshiping joyfully, preaching that Christ had ac-

tually come to lead believers to a perfect, sinless, everlasting life—the life of the spirit.

It was a noble and inspiring vision, and the Shakers had special services of worship and expression to accompany their urgent convictions about God, Christ, the devil and the world. Says Andrews in *The Gift to Be Simple:*

> The first believers were seized by such ecstasy of spirit that, like leaves in the wind, they were moved into the most disordered exercises running about the room, jumping, shaking, whirling, reeling, and at the same time shouting, laughing or singing snatches of song. No form existed: someone would impulsively cry out a line from the psalms, part of a hymn or a phrase—perhaps in an unknown tongue—bespeaking wild emotion; someone might prophesy; another would exhort his listeners to repentance.

The expression of faith which bloomed in the dancing, marching, singing, and religious drills that this group personified were emotional escape valves for the highly regimented, celibate, and strict taboos that the society adhered to. The believers coveted the simple virtues of plainness and honesty, sobriety and humility, chastity and escape from the snares of the world. The music they sang and the motions they used were often to "sweep the devil" out of their lives and out of the room. A clear equality of the sexes emerged, as did a sharp and constant separation from the world. Songs enforced the doctrine and codified the faith in a common way. One of the earliest and most popular was "Simple Gifts":

> 'Tis the gift to be simple,
> 'Tis the gift to be free,
> 'Tis the gift to come down
> Where we ought to be.
> And when we find ourselves
> In the place just right,
> 'Twill be in the valley of love and delight.

> When true simplicity is gained,
> To bow and to bend we shan't be ashamed,
> To turn, turn will be our delight,
> Till by turning, turning, we come round right.

One manuscript states that the song was "composed" by the Alfred Ministry June 28, 1948. It is a rather lively piece, Shaker Allegro in the original manuscript. (From *The Gift to Be Simple* by Edward D. Andrews.)

The Shaker influence reached out to affect numbers of families and the highest total membership was about 6,000 before the Civil War. Located in four major eastern communities, Dr. Edwards claims that "the Shakers represent the oldest, most successful, and most consistently pure communism in the new world, and their experiment in primitive Christianity has been replete with lessons of value to all mankind."

One of their Christmas songs, sometimes called a "war song," had these words to a simple tune:

> Behold it is a time of war
> And we have been enlisting,
> Emmanuel we're fighting for
> And Satan we're resisting
> We have not in this war begun
> To turn our backs as traitors
> But we will all unite as one
> Against our carnal natures.

And this one entitled "Dismission of the Devil":

> Be joyful, be joyful,
> Be joyful, be joyful,
> For Old ugly is going.
> Good ridance, good ridance,
> Good ridance we say
> And don't you never come here again.

Most of the inspired songs and sacred dances did not have

composers by name. They were ascribed to "spirits" which moved people to write and sing of their faith. Music was circulated privately between families and later by separate societies within the Shaker fellowship.

Other Traditions

During the Shaker period of religious development, other songs were composed that reflect this gentle spirit, this getting back to the simplicity of the gospel. Josiah Conder (1789–1855) wrote "Manna" and the words need little explanation.

> Day by day the manna fell.
> Oh to learn this lesson well!
> Still by constant mercy fed
> Give me, Lord, my daily bread.
> (This is associated with the tune "Mercy")
> JOSIAH CONDER

A man by the name of Jonathan Evans was also writing and composing during this colonial period. "Pisgah" is the tune usually joined with these words:

> Come, Thou soul-transforming Spirit,
> Bless the sower and the seed;
> Let each heart Thy grace inherit;
> Raise the weak, the hungry feed.
> From the Gospel, from the Gospel
> Now supply Thy people's need.
> JONATHAN EVANS

The Shaker influence and experiment in communism dwindled after the Civil War. Without marriage and children, the society had no realistic way to expand or even to continue. Converts and orphans did arrive from time to time, but today there are only several dozen believers remaining in the United States.

AMERICAN INDIAN MUSIC

It is unfortunate for non-Indians that so much of their

identification with native Americans and their music is related to the "war dance" which has appeared so often in
films and on television. Indeed, much of our popular knowledge concerning the Indian nations of North America is
based on slight fact and much fiction. Those close to the
Indian people know that their orientation and world-view
are deeply religious and filled with mysticism. The break-
down of Indian culture and the fragmentation of tribes by
western industrial influence have yet to diminish the linger-
ing aspects of their religious commitment. In many of the
present-day Indian youth movements there appears to be a
return to the religion of the Lodge and a sensitivity to old
ways and practices that reach back for thousands of years.

In the tribal communities that I have observed in Okla-
homa, New Mexico, and Arizona, Indian music is saturated
with religious overtones. Readers should be aware that the
members of the Navajo, Apache, Pueblo, and Hopi tribes
do not separate their lives in the manner of white people:
religion, art, music, employment, culture—rather all are
closely bound and interwoven in the fabric of existence.
The articles of handmade jewelry, the patterns and colors of
a blanket, the symbols found on pottery, the designs of sand
paintings, the chants of a rain dance, the presence of holy
mountains—all support and enforce a world-view that is
religious and mystical at the core. Not far from where I live
is the majestic sky city, the resident home of the Acoma
Indians in western New Mexico. One of their favorite songs
accompanied by dance goes:

> There in the west is the home of the raingods,
> There in the west is their water pool,
> In the middle of the water is the spruce tree
>   that they use as a ladder,
> Up from the water the raingods draw the crops
>   which give us life,
> East from there, on the place where we dance,
>   they lay the crops,

Then up from that place the people receive crops
and life.*

Most of the music that we know of in the American Indian
community is sung in groups. A major exception is the singing or chanting done by a medicine doctor seeking to assist
in a healing. In this instance, a sand painting is created, in
Navajo practice, as well as a song composed to aid the one in
need. In the group singing, accompaniment is on drums,
rattles, and sometimes a flute. Men lead in this liturgical
experience, women have a secondary part, joining in the
dancing and the singing.

Participation in Indian music is for all ages. Memory is
essential and a good voice is helpful but hardly a require-
ment. The special songs of the Pueblo tribes may be shared
with the Navajos and the other communities of the West.
There appears to be a great deal of similarity of sound and
meter—the differences showing in themes and style of dancing. Readers may be familiar with the Snake Dance, the
Corn Dance, the Buffalo Dance as well as the Kachina and
Butterfly Dance. Almost all of these dances with songs are
addressed to the deities, asking for help with the crops, the
arrival of rain, and the well-being of the people.

Many of the tribes who have been incorporated into the
Roman Catholic religious tradition continue to practice their
own dances, but in concert with the Christian liturgical year.
Hence, a famous dance in the southwest is the Reindeer,
which takes place around Christmas at Canoncito.

In some of the Navajo ceremonial dances the two favorite
themes are called Enemyway and Blessingway. The first deals
with protection from one's enemies, especially the threatening ghosts of the opposition. Blessingway has been called
"songs of hope" and consists of chants and songs for well-
being, good life, and the anticipations of happiness for preg-

---

* From Frances Densmore, *Music of Acoma, Isleta, Cochiti and Zuni
Pueblos* (Washington, D.C.: Smithsonian Institution, 1967), bulletin 165.

nant women. In the Navajo religion this is a primary doctrine of belief: Changing Woman is the leading deity of the tribe and the purification rites that are followed relate to the myth that man comes from woman and the cornbread powder performance is a symbolic bathing and drying of the life-giving deity.

Two illustrations which give some of the spirit and lyrics of Indian music are noted here:

THE SUN WORSHIPPERS

English version by
H.W. LOOMIS

United States - Zuni Indian

Rise,— a - rise,— a - rise!— (Rise, a - rise, a - rise!)

The dawn is here, day is call - ing thee. The

dawn is here; ev - er thank - ful be. Might - y

Day - god, he is watch - ing thee. Glo - rious

Life-god, he is guard-ing thee. _____

NAVAJO HAPPY SONG

U.S. Indian

With strong rhythm

Hi yo hi yo ip si ni yah, hi yo

hi yo ip si ni — yah, hi — yo hi yo ip si

(last time only)

ni yah, hi — yo hi yo ip si ni yah Ip si ri YAH!

A POPULAR JEWISH HYMN

The Jewish singing tradition predates all Christian music, tracing its start to the songs of celebration offered by Moses following the Exodus from Egypt. The Psalms of the Old Testament represented the central text to the music sung by Jews—and later Christians—for many centuries.

One hymn that is popular in Christian circles today can be traced to the fifteenth-century hymn that was used in Jewish worship: "Yigdal." It was produced by Daniel ben Juda, but known as the work of Moses ben Maimon (Maimonides), a rabbi of the twelfth century.

In 1770 Thomas Olivers, a Methodist clergyman, visited the Great Synagogue in London and heard the cantor sing "Yigdal." Olivers was so impressed with the hymn that he adapted it for use in the publication, *Wesley's Pocket Hymn-book* which appeared in 1785.

"The God of Abraham Praise" is currently used by both Jewish and Christian traditions, but it is historically and theologically a Hebrew melody dating back almost 1,000 years.

> The God of Abraham praise, All praised be his name,
> Who was, and is, and is to be, For aye the same!
> The one eternal God; ere aught that now appears;
> The First, the Last: beyond all thought His timeless
>   years!

MORAVIANS

A distinct feature of Moravian music is the trombone choir. It cannot be determined when their use was first introduced into the Moravian rite in Europe, but it is known that trombones were brought to this country by the immigrants to Georgia. They have continued in constant use ever since. The quartet, or choir, consists of treble, alto, tenor, and bass trombones, permitting the chorales to be played in full four-part harmony. Tradition has it that such chorales played in the early morning hours of Christmas Day, 1757, unwittingly deterred an attack by hostile Indians. A schedule of tunes was worked out in the mid-eighteenth century and later printed in the German Moravian Liturgy Book of 1791, which provided special chorales for each occasion in the life and worship of the community. Thus, "The Passion Chorale" tune by Hans Leo Hassler was used to announce the death of a member of the community. Such announcement tunes were played from the church tower. Another use was in the welcoming of distinguished visitors, such as General Washington and his retinue. It was an albeit rigorous service, and the trombonists gave long years of daily devotion to their duties. Rufus A. Grider, in *Historical Notes on Music in Bethlehem, Pennsylvania from 1741 to 1871,* has recorded the names of the players over a period of a century and a half.

An anecdote which he relates is illustrative of the liberal outlook toward music among the Moravians, in marked contrast with the New England viewpoint described in chapter two. When a zealous young minister questioned the propriety of using the same instruments in church on Sunday that had been used for secular music the evening before, one of his elders asked: "Will you use the same mouth to preach with today which you now use in eating sausage?"

Christian Science

Mary Baker Eddy not only developed the primary source-book for Christian Science, *Science and Health with Key to the Scriptures,* but also wrote at least seven hymns.

Three devotional hymns that are widely used in Christian Science services are:

Feed My Sheep

Shepherd, show me how to go
O'er the hillside steep,
How to gather, how to sow,
How to feed Thy sheep
I will listen for Thy voice,
Lest my footsteps stray;
I will follow and rejoice
All the rugged way.*

Mother's Evening Prayer

O gentle presence, peace and joy and power,
O life divine that owns each waiting hour,
Thou love that guards the nestling's faltering
    flight,
Keep Thou my child on upward wing tonight.

---

*Quotations from the words of Mary Baker Eddy are used with the permission of The Christian Science Board of Directors.

Communion Hymn

Saw ye my Savior?
Heard ye the glad sound?
Felt ye the power of the word?
'Twas the truth that made us free,
And was found by you and me
In the life and the love of our Lord.

Mourner, it calls you,
"Come to my bosom,
Love wipes your tears all away,
And will lift the shade of gloom,
And for you make radiant room
Midst the glories of one endless day."

Sinner, it calls you,
"Come to this fountain,
Cleanse the foul senses within;
'Tis the Spirit that makes pure,
That exalts thee, and will cure
All thy sorrow and sickness and sin."

Strongest deliverer,
Friend of the friendless,
Life of all being divine:
Thou the Christ, and not the creed;
Thou the Truth in thought and deed;
Thou the water, the bread, and the wine.

"Pass It On" is one of those gospel hymns which has attracted a broad following on both sides of the Atlantic,
probably through the travel experiences of the author, Henry
Burton.

Dr. Burton came from a devout Methodist family in
England, was to enter the ministry in the United States
following his studies at Beloit College. Amos Wells states
that Burton, in the 1860s, walked some 5,000 miles to gain
this advanced study. His parents and a family of twelve
lived on a farm in northern Illinois. In the early days of

his ministry, young Burton filled in for an ailing pastor in Wisconsin. This was followed by an assignment in Monroe, Wisconsin, for a minister who had entered the Civil War as a chaplain. Henry Burton's preaching was greeted with great excitement, the result being an evangelistic surge that brought more than fifty adult members into the congregation in less than six weeks.

Shortly after this ministry in America, Burton returned to England for more than forty years of preaching. He is best known in both countries for his hymns although many prize his contribution to *The Expositor's Bible,* in which he was responsible for the commentary on Luke.

Popular hymns of Dr. Burton include, "Break, Day of God," "There's a Light on the Mountains," and the hymn of the Wesley Guild, "Epworth." Burton also wrote "O King of Kings" for the famous composer, John Stainer.

In his volume *A Treasure of Hymns,* Amos R. Wells, the historian for the Christian Endeavor Society in 1914, disclosed this interesting correspondence with Dr. Burton regarding the development and inspiration for the hymn, "Pass It On."

> The incident which gave rise to the song was an experience of the Rev. Mark Guy Pearse, who is my brother-in-law; and I give it now in Mr. Pearse's own words: "Once when I was a schoolboy going home from the far-away little town in which I dwelt (Zeist, Holland), I arrived at Bristol, and got on board the steamer with just enough money to pay my fare; and that being settled, I thought in my innocence that I had paid for everything in the way of meals. I had what I wanted as long as we were in smooth water; then came the rough Atlantic, and the need of nothing more. I had been lying in my berth for hours wretchedly ill, and past caring for anything when the steward came and stood beside me.
>
> " 'Your bill, sir,' said he, holding out a piece of paper.

" 'I have no money,' said I, in my wretchedness.

" 'Then I shall keep your luggage. What is your name and address?' I told him. Instantly he took off the cap he wore, with the gilt band around it, and held out his hand. 'I should like to shake hands with you,' he said. Then came the explanation— how that, some years before, a little kindness had been shown his mother by my father in the sorrow of her widowhood. 'I never thought the chance would come for me to repay it,' he said pleasantly, 'but I'm glad it has.' As soon as I got ashore I told my father what had happened. 'Ah,' said he, 'see how a kindness lives! Now he has passed it on to you; and remember, if you meet anybody who needs a friendly hand, you must pass it on to him.' "

Such is the simple incident, which I first heard from the lips of my father-in-law, Mr. Mark Guy Pearse, of London, and it was his "Pass it on" which gave the inspiration and the title to my little song.

The words have had, to my knowledge, some sixteen different musical settings, but the most popular one in England is the one composed by your own Mr. George C. Stebbins, which has been sung by Gipsy Smith all round the world.

> Have you had a kindness shown?
>   Pass it on!
> 'Twas not given for thee alone—
>   Pass it on!
> Let it travel down the years,
> Let it wipe another's tears,
> Till in Heaven the deed appears,
>   Pass it on!
>
> Did you hear the loving word—
>   Pass it on!
> Like the singing of a bird?
>   Pass it on!

Let its music live and grow
Let it cheer another's woe,
You have reaped what others sow—
    Pass it on!

'Twas the sunshine of a smile—
    Pass it on!
Staying but a little while?
    Pass it on!
April beam, the little thing,
Still it wakes the flowers of spring,
Makes the silent birds to sing—
    Pass it on!

Have you found the heavenly light?
    Pass it on!
Souls are groping in the night,
    Daylight gone;
Hold thy lighted lamp on high,
Be a star in some one's sky,
He may live who else would die—
    Pass it on!

Love demands the loving deed;
    Pass it on!
Look upon thy brother's need,
    Pass it on!
Live for self, you live in vain;
Live for Christ, you live again;
Live for Him, with Him you reign—
    Pass it on!

All Hail the Power

Oliver Holden (1765–1844) was born in Shirley, Massachusetts. He served in the Marine Corps, and afterward settled in Charlestown, Massachusetts, which he helped to rebuild after its burning by the British. He became quite successful, acquired large real estate holdings, taught music and kept a music store, was elected to Congress, and became a prominent Mason. For a time he served as the minister of the Puritan church there which he had built virtually alone. His organ may be seen in the rooms of the Bostonian Society in the old state house in Boston.

His tune, "Coronation" (1793), is the oldest American tune now in general use. He intended that only tenor and bass voices would sing "Bring forth the royal diadem," and that the full choir would join in "And crown Him Lord of All."

What is sung today is a selection from Edward Perronet's original eight stanzas (1779) with revisions dictated by changing taste (although an earlier tune for the Perronet poem is still used in England).

The old-fashioned custom of "lining," by giving out a hymn line by line, probably caused the demise of this delicious stanza:

> Let high-born seraphs tune their lyre,
>   And as they tune it, fall
> Before His face who tunes their choir,
>   And crown Him Lord of all.

Like other innovations, or restorations, of the Oxord Movement, the choir procession was bitterly opposed in America, as well as in England. Although now a bit of English legend, the following anecdote could easily have been told of many American bishops: The story goes that at an Episcopal visitation to an English parish which was much under the influence of the Oxford Movement, the bishop refused to begin the service until the choir laid aside its processional cross. They are said to have retaliated by "revising" the opening hymn to:

> Onward, Christian soldiers,
>   Marching as to war,
> With the cross of Jesus
>   Left behind the door.

What a Friend We Have in Jesus

Joseph Scriven wrote the words (c. 1855). When asked by

a friend if he wrote the song, Scriven, born in Dublin and educated at Trinity College there, replied, "The Lord and I did it between us." Charles G. Converse's tune (1868) fits it well.

Ira D. Sankey relates this story in his *My Life and the Story of the Gospel Hymns:*

> Two men stood on a street in Port Hope, Ontario, when a man dressed in workingman's clothes, and carrying a wood saw and a sawhorse, passed them. One of the men spoke to him, and the other said, "Do you know that man? What is his name? I need someone to cut wood, and find it difficult to get a reliable man to do it."
>
> "But you can't get that man," was the reply. "That is Mr. Scriven. He won't cut wood for you."
>
> "Why not?" asked the first gentleman.
>
> "Because you are able to pay for it. He saws wood only for poor widows and sick people."

The man with the saw was Joseph Scriven, well known in the community for his benevolence and kindness. He was a true friend of the needy and distressed,* and he wrote the hymn that brings strength and comfort to thousands—to those who feel the press of poverty, as well as those whose physical needs are amply supplied.

The Hymns of Thanksgiving

Deep within our national and religious heritage are the Thanksgiving hymns. Only two or three are popular enough to have survived, hundreds have been written that have fallen out of general knowledge and use. One known to most is, "Come, Ye Thankful People, Come." Normally listed among harvest hymns, this was written by Henry Alford, British cleric and scholar who became the Dean of Canterbury in 1857. Alford wrote this before he gained that high office in

---

* Before Scriven came to Ontario, where he made his permanent home, his fiancée was drowned on the day before their wedding and from that day forward he devoted his life to Christ, and to helping those in need.

the Church of England. By conviction and personal persuasion, he was not a high churchman, enjoyed regular conversation and contacts with evangelicals and members of the nonconformist bodies. Alford stood, theologically, midway between Protestants and Roman Catholics. He wrote many hymns but "Come, Ye Thankful People, Come" is the one that survives in most of our hymnbooks.

> Come, ye thankful people, come,
> Raise the song of Harvest-Home!
> All is safely gathered in,
> Ere the winter storms begin:
> God, our Maker, doth provide
> For our wants to be supplied;
> Come to God's own temple, come,
> Raise the song of Harvest-Home!
>
> All the world is God's own field,
> Fruit unto His praise to yield;
> Wheat and tares together sown,
> Unto joy or sorrow grown:
> First the blade, and then the ear,
> Then the full corn shall appear:
> Lord of harvest, grant that we
> Wholesome grain and pure may be.
>
> For the Lord our God shall come,
> And shall take His harvest home;
> From His field shall in that day
> All offences purge away;
> Give His angels charge at last
> In the fire the tares to cast,
> But the fruitful ears to store
> In His garner evermore.
>
> Even so, Lord, quickly come
> To Thy final Harvest-Home!
> Gather Thou Thy people in,
> Free from sorrow, free from sin;
> There for ever purified,
> In Thy presence to abide:

Come, with all Thine angels, come,
Raise the glorious Harvest-Home!
                                HENRY ALFORD

Although this and other harvest hymns were written following the pilgrim experience in the New World and the saga surrounding the first Thanksgiving in Plymouth colony, they have become deeply engrained in our annual harvest celebration. It's interesting to note that in Cecil Northcott's fine study of popular hymns *Hymns We Love,* none of these songs were selected or chosen among the one hundred most favored. The reason, of course, is that his study covered British and Australian polls—and these religious communities do not share the same intensity of interest for Thanksgiving as does the American spirit. Strange, indeed, that a British Dean of Canterbury writes a song which is still highly beloved in our country, but almost unknown in his homeland.

Alford had an early feeling about his faith and his commitment to Christ. In childhood he was known to have written religious sentiments, and by eleven years of age he had compiled a selection of his own hymns. At sixteen, he jotted down this pledge:

> I do this day in the presence of God, and solemnly determine henceforth to become His and to do His work, as far as in me lied.

The work of God and the writing of Alford continues.

Out of the wars and tumults of the seventeenth century comes one of the most treasured harvest hymns. This was the period of The Thirty Years' War, which saw, among other things the forces of Holland and Spain locked in a long, fierce combat. While the battles were not that continuous, the conflict remained, and the struggle of Holland to be free from Spanish political power, and Catholic religious domination, was the primary reason for this extended warfare.

Out of this warring conflict, the Dutch were to gain enormous self-confidence and world-wide influence. Not only would the great ocean ventures and mercantile goals be pursued but the whole field of the arts, literature, and theology were launched with vigor and excitement. Many historians trace the rise of the Dutch as a global contender to the inspired leadership of Frederick Henry who came to the throne in 1625. This was the same year that "We Gather Together" was written; its source is traced to the folk songs of that period. It was not translated into English until Theodore Baker edited it in 1894.

There is some evidence that this hymn was sung by troops and townspeople following the end of a siege in Holland and victory for the Dutch. Popular tradition has the song being brought to these shores by the first pilgrims and connecting it with their celebrations following the first harvest. Whatever the official record, it is clear that this hymn now belongs to the harvest/religious events of Thanksgiving observations in the United States and Canada.

> We gather together to ask the Lord's blessing;
>   He chastens and hastens His will to make known;
> The wicked oppressing now cease from distressing,
>   Sing praises to His name; He forgets not His own.
>
> Beside us to guide us, our God with us joining,
>   Ordaining, maintaining His kingdom divine;
> So from the beginning the fight we were winning;
>   Thou, Lord, wast at our side; all glory be Thine!
>
> We all do extol Thee, Thou Leader triumphant,
>   And pray that Thou still our Defender wilt be.
> Let Thy congregation escape tribulation;
>   Thy name be ever praised! O Lord, make us free!
>   THEODORE BAKER

A powerful and popular harvest hymn of the Lutheran tradition came to America through the influence of Martin Rinkart (1586–1649). The beginning is also around the climactic events of the Thirty Years' War and the enormous thrust that Reformation theology had on music and liturgy in Germany and Europe at this time. "Now Thank We All Our God" was first used to sing the praises to God at the conclusion of the war and the signing of the Peace of Westphalia, 1648, the date for this hymn.

Scholars do not doubt the date of this hymn but believe that Rinkart composed it several years prior to this thrilling national celebration. What connected the hymn with Rinkart and the Peace signing was the fact that all regimental chaplains in the ranks of Frederick the Great were assigned this text on the preaching that observed the peace conference.

> And now let all praise God, who hath done great things, who hath glorified our days, and dealeth with us according to his loving kindness. He giveth joy to our hearts, that we may find peace in Israel as in the days of yore, thus He lets His loving-kindness remain with us, and He will redeem us in our day.
>
> Ecclesiasticus 50:22–24

It is difficult to imagine the horror and scenery of the Thirty Years' War. For years the constant movement of armies over the German countryside was so intense that orchards were completely destroyed, towns and villages obliterated and entire harvests ruined. Famine raged, disease was unending and the misery of the common man was almost unparalleled in Western history. Rinkart was a pastor in the heart of this sordid era. He lived in the community of Eilenberg, Saxony, his hometown in which he was later to be called as pastor by the council. For several months he was the solitary religious leader in this walled city, which later was a besieged fortress. On at least two occasions Rinkart saved the city from devastation by pleading with invading Swedish troops and lived to see the signing of the Peace of Westphalia—and the true faithful singing of this hymn, which many rank next to Luther's "A Mighty Fortress Is Our God."

Now Thank We All Our God

Now thank we all our God,
With hearts and hands and voices,
Who wondrous things hath done,
In whom His earth rejoices;
Who from our mother's arms
Hath blessed us on our way
With countless gifts of love,
And still is ours today.

O may this bounteous God
Through all our life be near us,
With ever joyful hearts
And blessed peace to cheer us;
And keep us in His grace,
And guide us when perplexed,
And free us from all ills,
In this world and the next.

All praise and thanks to God
The Father now be given,
The Son, and Him who reigns
With them in highest heaven;
The One eternal God,
Whom earth and heaven adore;
For thus it was, is now,
And shall be evermore!
                        MARTIN RINKART

It should be clear from the preceding account that the well of American religious hymns has been fed by many European springs and that the traditions of Christians everywhere have been firmly implanted in our soil and soul.

The Mormon Tradition

World-famous is the Mormon Tabernacle Choir of Salt Lake City, Utah. And just as renowned is the musical tradition that has sustained the development and growth of the Church of Jesus Christ of Latter-Day Saints. Before consid-

ering one of their most popular hymns, we should understand the perspective of their faith. In the preface of one of
their hymnals appears this concise statement:

> Within a few months of the organization of His
> restored Church, the Lord directed that Emma
> Smith, wife of the Prophet Joseph Smith, should
> make a selection of sacred hymns for use by the
> Saints in their worshiping assemblies. "My soul de-
> lighteth in the songs of the heart," said the
> Lord in this revelation. "Yea, the songs of the
> righteous is a prayer unto me, and it shall be an-
> swered with a blessing upon their heads." Since
> those early days the singing of sacred hymns has
> been an important part of the meetings in the
> Church of Jesus Christ of Latter-Day Saints.

One of the favored hymns, known to Mormons and non-
Mormons alike, is "Come, Come, Ye Saints."

> Come, come, ye Saints, no toil nor labor fear;
>   But with joy wend your way.
> Though hard to you this journey may appear,
>   Grace shall be as your day.
> 'Tis better far for us to strive
>   Our useless cares from us to drive;
> Do this, and joy your hearts will swell—
>   All is well! All is well!

Mormon historians have commented:

> Among members of the Church were inspired
> writers. Many of their songs were sung in times of
> joy and sorrow, cheering the Saints in their pioneer
> journeys, and strengthening them in their trials
> and tribulations. They became characteristic of the
> missionaries of the Church who traveled far and
> wide, and were a source of faith and consolation,
> encouragement, and strength. Today as they are
> sung they add fervor to our meetings, and provide
> inspiration for all who sing them or hear them
> sung.

5

Singing
a New Song to the Lord

"The composer is a man, like the painter and writer, observes the world around him and has something to say about it. If what he sees is beautiful, he seeks to rescue its beauty from oblivion in the way he knows best—through his music. If he is oppressed by what he sees and turns to God for consolation, he lifts up his soul to the Lord in music, his form of prayer."

JOHN DONALD ROBB
in *New Mexico Quarterly*

The old song of my spirit has wearied itself out
It has long ago been learned by heart;
It repeats itself over and over,
Bringing no added joy to my days or lift to my spirit.

I will sing a new song
I must learn the new song for the new needs.
I must fashion new words born of all the new growth of
    my life—of my mind—of my spirit
I must prepare for new melodies that have never been mine
    before,
That all that is within me may lift my voice unto God.

HOWARD THURMAN
in *The Mood of Christmas*

107

The Benefit of a Multiple Tradition

Anyone studying the religious music scene in North America quickly discovers the rivalries and crosscurrents that abound. Liturgical churchmen and those with advanced degrees in music support a different tradition of hymns and anthems. Those individuals within the conservative/Pentecostal/evangelistic branch of the church are strong advocates of another style and theology in hymns. What is sad for the whole Christian church is the belief held by some that we cannot appreciate the styles and tastes of others without losing the distinction of our own preference. Perhaps it can be done and is being done on a much wider plane than we appreciate.

At the beginning of the twentieth century Henry Date edited a hymnbook entitled *Pentecostal Hymns,* published by Hope Publishing Company, Chicago. Of the 300 pieces, Mr. Date made this comment in his introduction to the book:

> The aim has been to provide a book that would be broad enough in its scope to accommodate the needs of all departments of church and Sunday school work, except those that are met by an authorized hymnal. The latter book should always have preeminence. The peculiar needs of the Sunday school, the young people's prayer meeting, and the mid-week devotional service have been most carefully considered. The songs of an evangelistic character are a host. The classics, for which there are no substitutes in modern hymnody, have not been overlooked.

That is a generous summary of the music situation which has existed in the Christian church during this century. That Christian fellowship will be impoverished indeed which feels it can alleviate one tradition at the expense of another.

The Gospel Sounds Today

A large portion of music that is popular within the black

community and widely hailed by all people is simply called, gospel. Some of it is out of the jazz tradition of New Orleans, such as, "When the Saints Go Marching In"—originally a funeral song of celebration. Jazz was by origin black and southern. Before long, with the help of radio and a significant population center in Harlem, a widely received musical experience was reflected in the creativity of a culture. Dancing, the night-club ballroom experience, plus the Roaring Twenties, seasoned the music with all sorts of vibraticns—good and bad according to one's attitude on dancing, drinking, and places of entertainment.

Yet, the inroads of Prohibition and the criticism of church groups did not deter this American musical explosion. But the stunning popularity with the masses and the broad suspicion of the conservative churches did not favor a full appreciation for what was going on. Dr. Ahlstrom argues that there is a vital bridge linking "Steal Away to Jesus" and "The Saint Louis Blues." The living link was once the black author, William C. Handy, often called the "Father of the Blues." He was raised in a preacher's family— both father and grandfather were ministers. In his own life of composing, he alternated—as did the late Duke Ellington—between the sacred and the secular, the spirituals and the blues.

In 1941 William Handy was quoted as saying:

> I think rhythm is our middle name . . . When the darktown puts on its new shoes and takes off the brakes, jazz steps in. If it's the New Jerusalem and the River Jordan we're studying, we make the spirituals . . . In every case the songs come from way down deep . . . The dove descended on my head just as it descended on the heads of those guys who got happy at camp-meeting. The only difference was that instead of singing about the New Jerusalem my dove began to moan about brown women and the men they tied to their apron strings.
>
> WILLIAM C. HANDY
> from *Father of the Blues*

She was just another black kid growing up in New Orleans and singing "Jesus Loves Me This I Know" in Mt. Moriah Baptist Church. She believed the gospel, talked often about Dr. Jesus because she trusted his healing power—and along the way molded a style of religious music. A half century later she recorded "Silent Night," singing it in gospel style and a fervor like no other soloist, and the royalty check for the first year amounted to $25,000.

Her first choice was always gospel. When she was booked into the Newport Jazz Festival one summer, an Episcopal parish invited her to be in the morning worship service. When she accepted, the news panicked the promoters of the festival, "Giving away all that talent for nothing!" they said. When their groans of avarice reached her, she almost snarled, "Listen. Listen," said Mahalia Jackson, "When you stop singing free in church on Sunday, you are not a real gospel singer any more." All of this is reported in Laurraine Goreau's book, *Just Mahalia, Baby,* an exceptional Christian biography for those who believe that God uses the visions and pilgrimages of others to instruct his people.

In one chapter this conversation is reported. "He [a friend] just wanted to tell her again how wonderful she'd been, how remarkable "Silent Night" was; had everybody in church in tears. 'How do you do it?' he asked. Mahalia fixed the full force of her being on him. *'Don't you know?'* she said in disgust. This man had been around her all this much, and don't know her singing's from God."

In mid-career, Mahalia bought a home in Chatham Village, a Chicago suburb. The price was steep in this all-white neighborhood but Miss Jackson paid cash and moved in. Then came the bad mouthing from the people on the block, the foul letters, the obscene phone calls—even some guy with enough rage and insanity to shoot a bullet through her picture window. But she stayed and survived, and one afternoon she put up this plaque near the front door:

Dear Lord
In this House you are wanted and you are welcome

When she finished her Easter tour in Tokyo one spring, the gospel concert captivated her critics and fans alike. Wrote Hisamitsu Noguchi, dean of the drama critics:

> Her gospel songs have not only the perfect music beauty but also the very persuasive power by her belief . . . though I am not a Christian, I could not stop running tears—tears of joy.

Spirituals

Many musicians believe that the American spiritual is the most authentic expression of native tradition in the United States. Others argue for jazz, many more for country and western. Negro spirituals were the reflection of the life and mood of millions of people who labored under slavery in the United States. Howard Thurman, in his profound and helpful lectures at the Church for the Fellowship of All Peoples, San Francisco, published some central ideas relating to the origin and power of the spirituals. He suggests that the very texts of these handed-down songs were a vivid and correct interpretation of the social system with which these people were struggling.

As part of the preparation for understanding Negro spirituals, Dr. Thurman urges us to consider the place and message of the Negro preacher. For this man, above all others, gave "to the masses of his fellows a point of view which became for them a veritable Door of Hope . . . He was convinced that every human being was a child of God. This belief included the slave as well as the master."

Quite frankly, the slavery system in America or anywhere else in the world is a death system. Only the few pieces of hope, the spare fragments of aspiration, the borrowed convictions of trust and determination made it possible for generation after generation of Negroes to believe that their day would come, that one day Moses would tell old Pharaoh to "let my people go." Finally the Moses, Abraham Lincoln, did come and freedom painfully emerged—the songs of the country church and the theology of the Negro preacher and his flock were fulfilled. It was long and hard, and at times a terrifying struggle, but it never collapsed. The music is where many were salvaged. The mutuality and promise of the spiritual was lived over and over again in the black community.

Dr. Thurman, writing in *Deep River,* suggests that the Negro spirituals have three main sources: The Old and New Testaments; the world of nature about us; and the intensely personal experiences of religious/social encounters.

Much of the language and idiom of the people caught in slavery found identification with the bondage of the children of Israel as described in the Old Testament. Slave owners did not generally interfere with Negro worship and black preaching. The stories of the chosen people following Moses out of Egypt were the core theme that preachers and congregations returned to again and again. The parallel times seemed too close for chance: it was God's message to the slaves that they, like the Israelites, were in bondage to Egypt and so they sang in conviction and hope. The children were delivered.

> When Israel was in Egypt's land,
> Let my people go.
> Oppressed so hard they could not stand
> Let my people go.

> Refrain:
> Go down, Moses, way down in Egypt's land;
> Tell ole Pharaoh
> Let my people go.

> Thus saith the Lord, bold Moses said
> Let my people go
> If not I'll smite your first-born dead
> Let my people go.

> No more shall they in bondage toil,
> Let my people go
> Let them come out of Egypt's spoil
> Let my people go.

The Lord told Moses what to do,
Let my people go
To lead the children of Israel thro'
Let my people go.

When they had reached the other shore
Let my people go.
They sang a song of triumph o'er
Let my people go.

And they never stopped singing. When they came to the New Testament they were living with the Jesus experience. Thurman notes that very few spirituals deal with the advent of Christ. He tends to agree with James Weldon Johnson who observed that Christmas was more of a "wild celebration holiday" rather than a moment of deep religious bearing. Thurman also argues that the plantation owners probably played down the nativity stories (with the emphasis of Scripture on the righteousness of the poor and God's special caring for the deprived and captive). Indeed, the first sermon Jesus gave in Nazareth was to announce a powerful social message of deliverance. The southern slave holders may have bluntly deleted this from the Bibles of the black preachers.

If the whites wanted to edit Scripture, so did some blacks. Dr. Thurman recalls his regular youthful assignment of reading to his aged grandmother. In his Scripture readings he was instructed to read only the thirteenth chapter of First Corinthians—forget the rest of Paul's writings. "Why?" asked young Howard. His former slave grandmother said, "White plantation preachers are always using that Pauline text, 'Slaves be obedient to your masters.'" She vowed that if freedom ever came, that she would never read that part of the Bible.

There are some spirituals, though few, which did allude to Christ's birth. A favorite used in our time is:

When I was a seeker
I sought both night and day

> I asked de Lord to help me
> And He show'd me de way.
>
> Go tell it on de mountain
> Over hills and everywhere
> Go tell it on the mountain
> That Jesus Christ is born.

One aspect of the Negro spiritual that appeals to Dr. Thurman is its duality: the strong emphasis on the personal spiritual encounter with God and the vast, omnipotence of the heavenly Father that is above and beyond the creation and the creature. This is put in song in "Lily of the Valley":

> He's the lily of the valley
>   O my Lord
> He's the lily of the valley
>   O my Lord
> King Jesus in His chariot rides
>   O my Lord
> With four white horses side by side
>   O my Lord!

Again, Thurman writes in his *Deep River:*

> The most universally loved of all the hymns about Jesus is the well known "Were You There When They Crucified My Lord?"
>
> Some time ago when a group of Negroes from the United States visited Mahatma Gandhi, it was the song that he requested them to sing for him. The insight here is profound and touching. At last there is worked out a kind of identification in suffering which makes the cross universal in its deepest meaning. It cuts across differences of race, religion, class, and language and dares to affirm that the key to the mystery of the cross is found deep within the heart of the experience itself:
>
> "Were you there when they crucified my Lord?
> Were you there when they crucified my Lord?

> Oh, sometimes it causes me to tremble,
>   tremble, tremble,
> Were you there when they crucified my Lord?"

When we consider the variety and endurance of Negro spirituals, we realize what a large and powerful contribution they have been to the storehouse of religious music in America.

"Deep River" remains as one of the classic songs of faith—black or white. Thurman believes that this is the most intellectual of all Negro spirituals. It identifies the setting with sharp realism: the river represents the boundary of freedom. It may point to the Mississippi with all its presence and power through so many of the former Confederate states.

Others feel that it may be the river separating the United States and Canada. It has a biblical note: across the Jordan where John the Baptist preached repentance and where Jesus himself went to be baptized. It speaks of the Promised Land beyond the Jordan which even the leader and inspiration for freedom, Moses, did not get to inherit. There is a pilgrimage and a place. But "Deep River" looks almost beyond life into the far kingdom of God itself. Perhaps it was the only way to save one's sanity.

Concludes Thurman:

> For the slave, freedom was not on the horizon;
> there stretched ahead the long road down which
> there marched in interminable rows of cotton, the
> sizzling heat, the riding overseer with rawhide
> whip, the auction block when families were torn
> asunder, the barking of the blood-hounds, all of
> this, but no freedom.

But there was a faith, a preacher, a congregation, a song. It says then and now:

> Deep River, my home is over Jordan
> Deep River, my home is over Jordan.
> O, don't you want to go to that Gospel Feast

> That Promised Land where all is Peace?
> Deep River, I want to cross over into camp ground.

This projection of hope, this deep dream of faith for a better and safer and eternal place touched other songs sung by the slaves. "Michael Row de Boat Ashore" has much of the same warning and poignancy of message:

> Michael Row de boat ashore,
>   Hallelujah!
> Michael's boat a gospel boat,
>   Hallelujah!

And other verses strengthen the theme found in "Deep River"—a sense of life's ultimates:

> —Gabriel blow de trumpet horn
> —Jordan stream is wide and deep
> —Jesus stand on t'oder side
> —He raise de fruit for you to eat,
> —He dat eat shall never die,
> —Sinner row to save your soul.

Folk Hymns of the Southern Mountains

Much of the treasured music of the southern mountains is directly traced to the religious devotion of Christian families in England who settled in America and eventually clustered in the Southern Appalachia Mountains. Isolated and separated by the difficulties of transportation and communication, the religious communities preserved their tradition of what has come to be known as "white spirituals." Careful observers of the history and tradition of this area have noted the presence, to this day, of humming and chanting that marks the personality of these people.

"The Lily of the Valley" is an old English melody—a song that has continued to our time. My researcher and music historian friend, Anna Mary Bogue, suddenly produced the words from memory, recalling that her mother sang these lyrics years ago.

The Lily Of The Valley

In this same category of "white spiritual" is, "I'm a Poor Wayfaring Stranger," which one source describes in the following way:

> During the great revivals and camp meetings that spread from the Kentucky frontier after the Revolutionary War, many white spirituals appeared. They seem to have been influenced by Elizabethan modes and are usually best for solo voice, thereby differing from the Negro musical forms with their more exotic scales and ready harmonizations. The great folk-singer, Burl Ives, is responsible for the popularization (in the late nineteen-forties) of this spiritual, and is professionally billed as "The Wayfaring Stranger."

I am a poor wayfaring stranger,
A trav'ling through this world of woe,
Yet there's no sickness, toil, or danger
In that bright world to which I go.

Composer John Sweney incorporated this theme and mood in his work. He wrote and thought for a people that focused their faith on the future of God's kingdom. *Beulah* was their word for heaven and *sunshine* became the word for the inner radiance of Christian conviction in God's salvation. Sweney was to become well known in the late nineteenth century and his phrase "dove of peace" may have had Civil War overtones.

Beulah Land
WORDS: Edgar Page Stites

I've reached the land of corn and wine,
And all its riches freely mine;
Here shines undimmed one peaceful day,
For all my night has passed away.

Chorus:
O Beulah land, sweet Beulah land!
As on the highest mount I stand,
I look away across the sea
Where mansions are prepared for me,
And view the shining glory shore,
My heaven, my home for evermore.

My Savior comes and walks with me,
And sweet communion here have we,
He gently leads me by the hand,
For this is heaven's borderland.

A sweet perfume upon the breeze
Is borne from ever-vernal trees,
And flowers that never-fading grow
Where streams of life forever flow.

The zephyrs seem to float to me
Sweet sounds of heaven's melody,

As angels with the white-robed throng
Join in the sweet redemption song.

There's Sunshine in My Soul Today
MUSIC: C. 1887
WORDS: E. E. Hewitt

There's sunshine in my soul today,
  More glorious and bright
Than glows in any earthly sky,
  For Jesus is my light.

Chorus:
  Oh, there's sunshine, blessed sunshine
    When the peaceful, happy moments roll,
  When Jesus shows his smiling face,
    There is sunshine in my soul.

There's music in my soul today,
  A carol to my King,
And Jesus' listening can hear
  The songs I cannot sing.

There's springtime in my soul today,
  For when the Lord is near,
The dove of peace sings in my heart,
  The flowers of grace appear.

There's gladness in my soul today,
  And hope and praise and love,
For blessings which he gives me now,
  For joys laid up above.

New Songs of Faith

One of the happiest results of researching religious music is the revelation of new people and songs. Most of us are so caught up in our own tastes and traditions that we may not venture beyond the familiar and comfortable—or at least what measures up as traditional within our own religious preference. We forget that most of the songs we now sing were new at one time. Someone had to break out of old established patterns and risk censure, or at least a frown, when they introduced a new song or anthem.

Last Christmas a friend sent me a large greeting with this haunting message:

> I saw a stranger yestreen
> I put food in the eating-place
> Drink in the drinking-place
> Music in the listening-place
> And in the sacred name of the Triune
> He blessed myself and my house
> My cattle and my dear ones. . . .
> And the lark said in her song
>   Often, often, often
> Goes the Christ in the stranger's guise
>   Often, often, often
> Goes the Christ in the stranger's guise.*
>   OLD GAELIC RUNE

And that greeting, in old English print and surrounded with the colors of Christmas, went up on the nearest bulletin board, spreading a better word for the day ahead. Later I learned that this was from the collection of Alfred Burt Christmas carols and the song is entitled, "Christ in the Stranger's Guise." This collection of contemporary carols, and a superb representation of what is happening in Christian music, has a background that is both educational and inspiring. Wrote Fred Bock:

> A few years ago, my friend, Lex deAzevedo, invited me to a Christmas party that turned out to be the highlight of my Christmas season. The spirit of Christmas was in the air, the lights on the Christmas tree were bright and exciting, the short talk on the meaning of Christ's birth in our present day and age was both uplifting and inspiring . . . but the music! This was the first time that I had ever

---

*Original music by Alfred Burt. Words based on a traditional poem. TRO © 1954 and 1957 Hollis Music, Inc. New York, N.Y. Used by permission.

heard the Alfred Burt Christmas Carols, and it was
an evening long to be remembered. I never knew
Alfred Burt, for he had died of cancer several years
earlier, but through Lex, I had met Al's wife, Anne,
and his daughter, Diane. Anne and Diane Burt are
so very proud of Al's writings, and justly so! The
Burt Carols become more and more famous each
year, as all over the world people are starting to
sing "Caroling, Caroling," and "Some Children See
Him," right along with "White Christmas" and
"Silent Night."

The story of how the Burt Carols came into being is an interesting one: it started a long time ago
when Al's father, an Episcopal clergyman, began
the family tradition. He would spend weeks and
months writing the single new carol for the year.
This new carol was to be the Burt family's Christmas card for the season. It was the high point of the
year for everyone. After the death of Al's father,
Anne and Al continued the tradition. The party
that Lex invited me to was the annual King Sisters'
Christmas Party (Alyce King is Lex's mom) and the
highlight of the evening was when we all gathered
in the living room—most everyone chose to sit on
the floor—and sang the Burt Carols. O, we also sang
"Hark, the Herald Angels Sing," "Winter Wonder-
land," and even the "Hallelujah Chorus" (without
music) but the true climax of the evening was the
Burt Carols.

You have a treat in store for you! If you have
heard these carols you know what I mean. And if
you have not heard the Alfred Burt Christmas
Carols, listen carefully, and expect yourself to be
lifted right to the heart of the Christmas Spirit.

Three of the most popular new songs in Christian hymnbooks today are "Morning Has Broken," "Lord of the
Dance," and "They'll Know We Are Christians by Our
Love." I would also include Kurt Kaiser's, "Pass It On," as
representative of the creative surge in Christian music.

Morning Has Broken
WORDS: Eleanor Farjeon 1931
MUSIC: Gaelic Melody
ARR. by David Evans 1927

Morning has broken like the first morning,
Blackbird has spoken like the first bird.
Praise for the singing!
Praise for the morning!
Praise for them, springing fresh from the Word!

Sweet the rain's new fall, sunlit from heaven,
Like the first dewfall on the first grass.
Praise for the sweetness
Of the wet garden,
Spring in completeness where His feet pass.

Mine is the sunlight! Mine is the morning
Born of the one light Eden saw play!
Praise with elation,
Praise Every morning,
God's re-creation of the new day!*

Lord of the Dance
WORDS: Sidney Carter 1963
MUSIC: Based on a Shaker tune
ARR. and adapted by Sidney Carter

I danced in the morning when the world was begun.
And I danced in the moon and the stars and the sun,
And I came down from heaven and I danced on earth—
At Bethlehem I had my birth.

Dance, then, wherever you may be
I am the Lord of the Dance, said he,
And I'll lead you all, wherever you may be,
And I'll lead you all in the dance, said he.**

*Used by permission of the executors of the estate of the late Eleanor
Farjeon. It was first published by Oxford University Press.
**© 1963 by Galliard Ltd. All rights reserved. Used by permission of
Galaxy Music Corp., New York, sole U.S. agent.

They'll Know We Are Christians by our Love

Words and Music

Peter Scholtes 1966

We are one in the Spirit
We are one in the Lord,
We are one in the Spirit,
We are one in the Lord.
And we pray that all unity may one day be restored.
And they'll know we are Christians by our love,
    by our love,
Yes, they'll know we are Christians by our love.

We will walk with each other,
We will walk hand in hand,
We will walk with each other,
We will walk hand in hand.
And together we'll spread the news that God is in our land,
And they'll know we are Christians by our love,
    by our love,
Yes, they'll know we are Christians by our love.*

A close study of these hymns reveals a sharp sensitivity to the large concerns of our day: an appreciation for the beauty and worth of all creation; a cosmic grasp of the power and design of the universe under God's providence; and a new awareness of the religious values of the arts.

Many of us have pled for "space hymns." Our hymnals are filled with solid notes about earth, wave, and water but rather thin or totally absent with references to the new frontier of the universe. Richard C. Trench has written this work which merits our "space recognition."

If there had anywhere appeared in space
    Another place of refuge where to flee,
Our hearts had taken refuge in that place,
    And not with Thee.

For we against creation's bars had beat
    Like prison'd eagles; through great worlds

---

*© 1966 by F.E.L. Publications, Ltd. 1925 Pontius, Los Angeles, California. Used by permission.

>   Had sought but a foot of ground to
>   plant our feet
>   Where Thou wert not.

>   And only when we found in earth and air,
>   In heaven or hell, that such might nowhere be,
>   That we could not flee from Thee anywhere,
>   We fled to Thee.
>   Richard C. Trench

As Howard Thurman declares, we must sing a new song to fit our new lives, our fresh thoughts, our latest dreams. Within the American community there are many causes, many challenges that are worthy of new songs of faith. Let us believe that our heritage is deep and strong to sponsor countless new songs which are signs of hope in the next two hundred years.